GIC
mits

DATE DUE

~~MR 1 0 '99~~			
~~MY 1 7 01~~			
~~JE 2 04~~			
~~AP 1 8 03~~			
~~DE 1 9 08~~			
~~JA 2 6 09~~			
~~FE 1 2 09~~			
~~JE 1 0 09~~			

DEMCO 38-296

FORMAL LOGIC
Its Scope and Limits

Third Edition

Richard Jeffrey

Professor of Philosophy
Princeton University

McGraw-Hill, Inc.

New York St. Louis San Francisco Auckland Bogotá
Caracas Lisbon London Madrid Mexico Milan
Montreal New Delhi Paris San Juan Singapore
Sydney Tokyo Toronto

This book was set in Times Roman.
The editors were Cynthia Ward and Margery Luhrs;
the production supervisor was Leroy A. Young.
The cover was designed by David Romanoff.
R. R. Donnelley & Sons Company was printer and binder.

FORMAL LOGIC
Its Scope and Limits

34567890 DOC DOC 95432

ISBN 0-07-032357-7

Library of Congress Cataloging-in-Publication Data

Jeffrey, Richard C.
    Formal Logic: Its Scope and Limits/Richard Jeffrey.—3rd ed.
       p.   cm.
    Includes bibliographical references and index.
    ISBN 0-07-032357-7
    1. First-order logic.   I. Title.
BC128.J43   1991
160—dc20   90-21013

For Jane and Mark

CONTENTS

Chapter 3   Generality   **35**

Chapter 4   Multiple Generality   **59**

PREFACE

This is a book for beginners, designed to familiarize them with a formal system of first-order logic in the course of a semester's study and give them access to the discoveries defining the scope and limits of formal methods that marked logic's coming of age in the twentieth century: Gödel's completeness and incompleteness theorems for first- and second-order logic, and the Church–Turing theorem on the undecidability of first-order logic.

The formal system (the tree method) is based on Evert Beth's method of semantic tableaux, or, equivalently, Jaakko Hintikka's method of model sets. In contrast to the so-called natural deduction methods, whose vogue in elementary logic texts began in 1950, the tree method is thrillingly easy to understand and use. It is this simplicity that lets students get control of the nuts and bolts of formal logic in a couple of months, so that there is time in the semester for the more abstract topics treated in the last three chapters and at the ends of Chapters 2 through 6.

This third edition is generally rewritten and reorganized, to combine the accessibility of the first edition with the depth of the second. The tree method is elaborated in manageable steps over five chapters, in each of which its adequacy is reviewed; soundness and completeness proofs are extended at each step, and the decidability proof is extended at the step from truth functions to the logic of nonoverlapping quantifiers with a single variable, after which undecidability is demonstrated by example. The first three chapters are bilingual, with arguments presented twice, in logical notation and in English; formal translation drill comes in Chapters 4 and 5, with multiple quantification and identity. The book consists of six chapters of scope, then three chapters of limits. I've tried to prove the facts about scope and limits clearly and memorably, with a minimum of fuss, without cutting corners.

After the first, introductory chapter, the book is one straight argument, with a minimum of excursion. There's nothing here about functional completeness, probability, block diagrams, or deduction trees, as there was in the second edition. (That material does appear in the instructor's manual along with other oddments, and can be recycled as handouts.) Other bits of the chapters of the second edition called "Truth-Functional Equivalence" and "Conditionals" appear more compactly here in Chapter 1. The "undecidability" chapter of the second edition has split in two here: uncomputability, then undecidability. The "Completeness and Incompleteness" chapter has also split; here, completeness of the method is proved in bits as the method grows in Chapters 2 through 6, and the unformalizability of second-order logic gets a chapter to itself, at the end, where it's derived from the undecidability of first-order logic and the existence of a routine for associating with any first-order argument a second-order argument that's valid if and only if the first is invalid.

Again I am indebted to many users of the book for help in shaping this edition, and again my main debt is to George Boolos, my main meta-mathematician, who is really a coauthor. (But the actual text is mine, and even contains bits that George deprecates.) The present shape of Chapter 9 stems from a suggestion of Richard White's. George told me how to do it, and Lisa Downing kept me rewriting my versions of it so that it's now pretty clear. Chapter 7 incorporates a suggestion of Sam Wheeler's. All have provided advice and corrections elsewhere in the book, as have John Burgess, Eric Steinhauer, Philip Kitcher, Mark Hinchliff, and others whom I'm forgetting. Thanks to all.

The book is lovingly dedicated to my mother and to the memory of my father, whose jovial sophisms drove me into logic in the first place.

Richard Jeffrey

1
TRUTH-FUNCTIONAL LOGIC

Formal logic is the science of deduction. It aims to provide systematic means for telling whether or not given conclusions follow from given premises, i.e., whether arguments are valid or invalid. This book shows how that aim is partly attainable, and why it is not fully attainable.

Validity is easily defined:

> A **valid** argument is one whose conclusion is true in every case in which all its premises are true.

Then the mark of validity is absence of counterexamples, cases in which all premises are true but the conclusion is false.

Difficulties in applying this definition arise from difficulties in canvassing the cases mentioned in it. In the "truth-functional" arguments to which we now turn, these difficulties are at a minimum. Here, cases are simply possibilities as to joint truth and falsity of sentences out of which the premises and conclusion are formed. Within this division of the subject, the aim of logic is fully and simply attainable, for routine methods allow us to determine whether an argument is truth-functionally valid or not.

1.1 "NOT," "AND"

"Min is not both home and on board. She's home. Therefore she's not on board." That three-sentence argument is truth-functionally valid. The first two sentences are its premises, and the word "therefore" flags its conclusion. We write it like an arithmetic problem, with premises adding up to the conclusion:

Premise:	Min's not both home and on board.	Not (*A* and *B*)
Premise:	She's home.	*A*
Conclusion:	She's not on board.	Not *B*

(In the schematic version, "*A*" says that Min is home, "*B*" that Min is on board.)

A counterexample would be a case in which both premises are true and the conclusion is false. Let's think about how that could happen. To make the second premise true, "*A*" would have to be true—Min would have to be home. To make the conclusion false, "*B*" would have to be true—Min would have to be on board. Then the part "*A* and *B*" of the first premise, the part "Min's both home and on board," would be true, and the whole first premise, "not (*A* and *B*)," would be false—not true, as in a counterexample. Then there are no counterexamples. The argument is valid.

In effect we have surveyed the four possibilities as to truth (t) and falsity (f) of "*A*" and "*B*"—efficiently—and found that none of them is a counterexample. In a straightforward, inefficient search, those cases might be listed as at the left of the following truth table, under "*AB*." The three column headings at the right are the premises and conclusion of the argument, and the columns of "t"s and "f"s under them are the truth values they assume in the four cases.

	AB	Not (*A* and *B*)	*A*	Not *B*
Case 1	tt	f (t)	t	f
Case 2	tf	t (f)	t	t
Case 3	ft	t (f)	f	f
Case 4	ff	t (f)	f	t

In parentheses under "and" are the truth values of the part "Min is both home and on board" (*A* and *B*) of the second premise. That part is true in case 1, where *AB* is tt, and false in the other three cases, where "*A*" is false or "*B*" is. The truth values of the full second premise are listed under "not" in the next column to the left. "Not" has the effect of changing t to f and f to t both there and in the rightmost column, which derives from the column under "*B*" at the left. Having completed those computations, one would back off and see whether the following counterexample pattern appears in any case:

	AB	Not (*A* and *B*)	*A*	Not *B*
Case *n*	??	t	t	f

A survey of the four rows of the truth table shows that there is no such case, no counterexample, and so the argument is valid.

Our first, efficient search cut through the work of constructing the whole table. We observed that only the case in which "*A*" and "*B*" are both *t* (case 1) could be a counterexample, and then observed that the first premise is false in that case, so it's no counterexample after all.

1.2 "OR"

Min is home or on board. Henry is home or Min is. Min is not home. That's all we know. What follows about where they are?

Here we have three premises in search of a conclusion. If we use "*A*" and "*B*" as in Section 1.1 and use "*C*" for "Henry is home," the argument has the following shape:

Premise:	Min is home or Min is on board.	*A* or *B*
Premise:	Henry is home or Min is home.	*C* or *A*
Premise:	Min is not home.	Not *A*
Conclusion:	?	?

Can all three premises be true? What if they are?

For "not *A*" to be true, "*A*" must be false. Now an "or" sentence can't be true if both parts are false, so with "*A*" false, the first premise can't be true if "*B*" is false, and the second can't be true if "*C*" is false. Then "*B*" and "*C*" are both true. We know all: Min is on board, Henry is home. If we fill in the question marks as follows, the argument will be valid:

Conclusion:	Min is on board and Henry is home.	*B* and *C*

That was an efficient analysis of the problem. A straightforward, inefficient approach would have canvassed the eight cases regarding *ABC* enumerated at the left of the following truth table. In effect, our efficient approach cut out the first four cases, where the third premise, "not A," is false—cases that can't be counterexamples no matter how the truth values of the other premises fall out. But instead of computing the t's and f's in the lower half of the table, the efficient analysis homed straight in on the ftt case for ABC (case 5 below) as the one that makes all premises true.

	ABC	A or B	C or A	Not A	Conclusion
Case 1	ttt			f	The conclusion
Case 2	ttf			f	must be t in
Case 3	tft			f	case 5 if the
Case 4	tff			f	argument is
Case 5:	ftt	t	t	t	to be valid.
Case 6	ftf	t	f	t	Its truth value
Case 7	fft	f	t	t	in other cases
Case 8	fff	f	f	t	doesn't matter.

1.3   IS THIS ARGUMENT VALID?

"Min is home or on board, so is Henry, neither is on board, so they're both home." (Schematically, the premises are "A or B," "C or D," "not B and not D," and the conclusion is "A and C.") Do this one efficiently; the truth table has 16 rows. For help, see the solution below.*

1.4   A BAD ARGUMENT

MORIARTY: "She can't be home, because we know she's home or on board, and I've just learned that she's on board."
THIN: "Do we know that she doesn't *live* on board?"
MORIARTY: "Oh-oh."

Moriarty stated his conclusion first ("She can't be home"), then gave his reasons ("because ..."). When Thin's question suggested that so far as we know she might be both home and on board, Moriarty backed down. Let's see why. This was his argument:

She's home or on board.	A or B
She's on board.	B
She's not home.	Not A

---

* If the third premise is true, "B" and "D" are both false. Then truth of the first two premises (the "or" sentences "A or B," "C or D") requires truth of "A" and of "C." But then the conclusion "A and C" is true, and so no case is a counterexample; the inference is valid.

In a counterexample premise "*B*" would be true, and "*A*" would be true because the conclusion would be false. Then a counterexample exists or not depending on whether or not the first premise was meant to be compatible with Min's being both home and on board; the argument is valid if the "or" was meant in an exclusive sense ("*A* or *B* but not both"), invalid if not.

Thin's question made Moriarty realize ("Oh-oh") that what we knew to begin with was only that Min was home or on board, not that she was home or on board but not both. The first premise is true on a nonexclusive interpretation of "or," but on that interpretation the argument is invalid. On the exclusive interpretation the argument is valid but the first premise goes beyond what we know. Either way, it's a bad argument.

1.5 SOUNDNESS

Arguments from false premises are defective even if valid, and even if their conclusions are true. An example is "Sharks are mammals, so whales or sharks are mammals." That argument is valid but unsound.

A **sound** argument is one that's valid and has no false premises.

It is soundness of an argument that ensures truth of the conclusion; mere validity carries no such guarantee, nor does mere truth of all premises. An argument can be unsound because not all premises are true or because the conclusion doesn't follow—and that's not an exclusive "or."

In the definition of soundness, "truth" means truth in reality, in the actual case, which is what the word means in common English. In reality, "Whales are mammals" (*A*) is true (t) and "Sharks are mammals" (*B*) is false (f).

	AB	*A* or *B*
Case 1	tt	t
Case 2 (actual):	tf	t
Case 3	ft	t
Case 4	ff	f

Throughout this book, when we speak of truth simply (not of truth in case such-and-such), we mean truth in the ordinary sense. Use of fanciful examples makes it easy to overlook simple truth and falsity. Does Min really live on board? There is no fact of the matter. To illustrate soundness and unsoundness we must use real examples, from life.

1.6 "IF"

The following argument is immediately recognizable as valid by people who have never heard of counterexamples. That's good because as yet we don't know how the truth values of "if" sentences are affected by the truth values of their components. Granted the validity of this argument, we can discover something about that.

| If Min works on board that leaky tub, she's underpaid. | If A, B |
Min works on board that leaky tub.	A
She's underpaid.	B

As the argument is valid, there is no case concerning the truth values of "A" and "B" that makes "If A, B" and "A" true and "B" false. What we've discovered is that in the tf case for AB, the sentence "If A, B" isn't true, it's false:

AB	If A, B
tf	f

The fragmentary information just obtained about "if" is enough to establish validity of the argument from the premises "Damned if you do, damned if you don't" to the obvious conclusion. Premises and conclusion can be rewritten as below without changing the sense. Truth values in any counterexample would be as shown at the right.

| If you do, you're damned. | If A, B | t |
If you don't, you're damned.	If not A, B	t
You're damned.	B	f

But those truth values can't arise, for if the conclusion "B" is false then one premise or the other must be false according to our fragmentary information about "if." (Either "A" or "not A" has to be true, so either "If A, f" or "if not A, f" has to be false.)

1.7 DENIAL, CONJUNCTION, DISJUNCTION

Now let's pause to establish some useful terminology and notation.

Connectives are grammatical devices that operate on sentences to produce new sentences. Examples already encountered are denial, conjunction, disjunction, and conditioning, corresponding to use of the English words "not," "and," "or," and "if." The uses we shall focus on are truth-functional, i.e., the truth values of the new statements they produce are determined by the truth values of the statements on which they operate.

Denials are formed by prefixing the word "not" ("Not everyone dances"), by infixing it ("Min is not home"), and in other ways ("7 + 5 ≠ 11"). A uniform, cumbersome method is to prefix the phrase "It is false that" or "It is not the case that." In logical notation we form denials by prefixing the sign "¬."

Conjunctions can be formed by infixing "and" or "but" or a comma, and in other ways. In logical notation we infix the sign " ∧ ." Thus, with "*A*" and "*B*" as statements that Min is home and Min is on board, and "*C*" and "*D*" as corresponding statements about Henry, English would go over into logical notation as follows:

Min is home and on board.	$A \wedge B$
Min is home, so is Henry.	$A \wedge C$
Min is home but Henry's on board.	$A \wedge D$

English can use the difference between "but" and "and" to clarify grouping as in (1) below, and can use "both" with "and" as in (2) and (3) to indicate grouping that logical notation shows with parentheses.

1.	Min is not home but on board.	$\neg A \wedge B$
2.	Min is not both home and on board.	$\neg(A \wedge B)$
3.	Min is not both home and on board, she's at work.	$\neg(A \wedge B) \wedge W$

Disjunctions are "or" statements that aren't intended in an exclusive sense. When the exclusive sense is meant here, there will be an indication to that effect, but unqualified "disjunction" will always mean the nonexclusive kind. In logical notation, truth values of disjunctions are indicated by the sign " ∨ ," as in the following two examples, which illustrate two ways in which colloquial English indicates grouping without using parentheses:

4.	Min and Hen are home or Min's on board.	$(A \wedge C) \vee B$
5.	Either Min's home and Hen's on board or Min's on board.	$(A \wedge D) \vee B$

In (4), English gets the effect of parentheses "$(A \wedge C)$" by combining "Min is home" ("*A*") and "Hen is home" ("*C*") into a sentence with a compound subject: "Min and Hen are home." In (5), where that device would be awkward, colloquial English identifies the first component of the disjunction by bracketing it with "either ... or." There the word "either" is used as a sign of grouping in a disjunction that we take to be nonexclusive until proved otherwise.

For the most part "or" statements are disjunctions (nonexclusive ones), as when someone honestly says "Min's home or on board" without knowing which and without meaning to rule out the possibility that she lives on board. In English we may indicate the exclusive sense by stressing the word "or" by loudness (6) or repetition (7) or by explicitly adding the disclaimer "but not both" to the nonexclusive disjunction (8).

6. Min is home OR on board.

7. She's home or on board, one or the other.

8. She's home or on board but not both. $(A \lor B) \land \neg(A \land B)$

1.8 CONDITIONALS

Conditionals are "if" statements. In logical notation we form them by writing " $\rightarrow$ " between two statements, viz., the antecedent (before the arrow) and the consequent (after the arrow). In the following five examples the antecedent (A) is "Min is home" and the consequent (C) is "Henry is home"—even where it doesn't look that way. The uniform logical notation "$A \rightarrow C$" highlights that.

1. If Min is home then Henry is.   If A then C $A \rightarrow C$

2. If Min is home, Henry is.   If A, C $A \rightarrow C$

3. Henry is home if Min is. C if A $A \rightarrow C$

4. Min is home only if Henry is. A only if C $A \rightarrow C$

5. Only if Henry is home is Min home.   Only if C A $A \rightarrow C$

In (1), (2), and (3), "if" flags the logical antecedent, even where that comes second in English as in (3). Adding "only" (4) and (5) changes that; "only if" flags the logical consequent even where that comes first in English, as in (5). It's obvious that the first three come to the same thing, and that the last two do. It's less obvious that all five come to the same thing.

That's because we naturally read these statements as general information about Min and Henry's habits [(4) and (5)] or as consequences of such information [(1), (2), and (3)]. But (4) and (5) don't state such information explicitly. An explicit statement would look something like (6) below. From that, an explicit version of (1) follows (statement 7):

6. Any time Min is home   *At any time* x (*Min is home at* x $\rightarrow$
   is a time Henry is home.   *Henry is home at* x)

7. If Min is home now   *Min is home now* $\rightarrow$
   then Henry is home now.   *Henry is home now*

Statements 1 through 5 are to be read as claims about the couple's present whereabouts. Those claims need not be based on any such general information as (6), but may spring from special features of the present occasion, e.g., that Min left home this morning without her key. Read in that light, (1) through (5) may be seen as five ways of saying that in fact, as matters stand now, Min isn't home unless Hen is—five ways of denying that Min is home but Hen isn't.

If that's so, these always agree in truth value:

8. $A \to B \qquad \neg(A \wedge \neg B)$

Since the second of these is false in the tf case for AB and is otherwise true, this completes the fragmentary information that "$A \to B$" is false in case "A" is true and "B" is false, obtained in Section 1.6. We now know that in the other three cases regarding the truth values of "AB," "$A \to B$" is true.

1.9 COUNTERFACTUAL CONDITIONALS

"Hen is home if Min is" might be called a matter-of-fact conditional in contrast to so-called counterfactual conditionals like "Hen would be home if Min were." It's matter-of-fact conditionals that we're mainly concerned with in science, mathematics, and everyday talk. They are what we refer to in this book simply as "conditionals," and symbolize with arrows.

Here is another contrasting pair, from real life:

1. If Oswald hadn't killed Kennedy, someone else would have.

2. If Oswald didn't kill Kennedy, someone else did. $\qquad (\neg O \to S)$

The conditional (1) is called counterfactual because its mode of statement suggests that the "if" part concerns a condition contrary to fact: "Granted that Oswald did kill Kennedy, if he hadn't, someone else would have." There is no such suggestion in the matter-of-fact conditional (2).

Clearly, (1) and (2) make different statements. That's clear because (1) is probably false, but (2) is surely true. And while it's plausible to analyze the matter-of-fact conditional (2) as a version of the disjunction

3. Oswald or someone else killed Kennedy $\qquad (O \vee S)$

the counterfactual conditional (1) isn't even truth-functional; it's not doubt about the truth values of the components "Oswald didn't kill Kennedy" (false) and "Someone other than Oswald killed Kennedy" (false) that makes us unsure about the truth value of (1).

A postscript about conditionals (i.e., matter-of-fact ones): if (2) and (3) really do come to the same thing, then we have another route to the conclusion of Section 1.8. Since (2) is false exactly when (3) is, i.e., when "O" and "S" are both false, the conditional "$\neg O \to S$" is false exactly then, i.e., when its antecedent ("$\neg O$") is true and its consequent is false. Then if (2) and (3) come to the same thing, the f case for conditionals discovered in Section 1.6 is the only one; "If A then B" is false in the tf case for AB, true in the tt, ft, and ff cases.

1.10 BICONDITIONALS AND LOGICAL EQUIVALENCE

The conjunction of the conditionals "C if A" and "C only if A" comes out more briefly as "C if and only if A"—and still more briefly as "C iff A" in common mathematical shorthand. In logical notation we write that as "$A \leftrightarrow C$." The biconditional "$A \leftrightarrow C$" says that "C" is true if "A" is and vice versa; i.e., it says that $(A \rightarrow C) \wedge (C \rightarrow A)$.

   When is the biconditional true? *Answer:* When its two component sentences are *equivalent*, i.e., *equi* ("same") *valent* ("value"), same in truth value. That's sameness of truth value in fact, in the actual case. If the agreement extends to all cases, we speak of *logical* equivalence, equivalence not just in fact but as a matter of logic.

> Sentences are said to be **logically equivalent** when they have the same truth values in all cases.

Example: At the end of Section 1.9, "(2) and (3) come to the same thing" means that (2) and (3) are logically equivalent.

1.11 RULES OF VALUATION

These are rules for computing the truth values of denials, conjunctions, disjunctions, conditionals, and biconditionals:

> $\neg$ Denial reverses truth value.
> $\wedge$ Conjunctions are true if all components are true, false if any are false.
> $\vee$ Disjunctions are true if any components are true, false if all are false.
> $\rightarrow$ Conditionals with true antecedents and false consequents are false, all others are true.
> $\leftrightarrow$ Biconditionals are true if their two components agree in truth value, false if they disagree.

Here are some of the corresponding truth tables:

A	$\neg A$	AB	$A \wedge B$	$A \vee B$	$A \to B$	$A \leftrightarrow B$	ABC	$A \wedge B \wedge C$	$A \vee B \vee C$
t	f	tt	t	t	t	t	ttt	t	t
f	t	tf	f	t	f	f	ttf	f	t
		ft	f	t	t	f	tft	f	t
		ff	f	f	t	t	tff	f	t
							ftt	f	t
							ftf	f	t
							fft	f	t
							fff	f	f

These are only some of them, because there are also 16-case tables for "$A \wedge B \wedge C \wedge D$" and "$A \vee B \vee C \vee D$," 32-case tables when "$E$" is added, and so on without end. The number of cases doubles every time the number of letters increases by 1. (When a new letter is introduced, the old block of cases is duplicated, first with a "t" in front, then with an "f.") The verbal rules of valuation are clearer than truth tables, and more general.

Number of letters: $n = 1 \quad 2 \quad 3 \quad 4 \quad 5 \quad 6 \quad \dots \quad 10$
Number of cases: $2^n = 2 \quad 4 \quad 8 \quad 16 \quad 32 \quad 64 \quad \dots \quad 1024$

1.12 ODDITIES OF "IF"

Our focus is on truth and falsity. We are not concerned with the purpose of making a statement (to inform, mislead, amuse, threaten, etc.) or even with how or whether the speaker knows that what's said is true. It is the job of formal logic to point out that if it's true that Dick did it, then it's equally true that Tom, Dick, or Harry did it. But it is not the job of formal logic to point out that to make the second statement while knowing that the first is also true may be to mislead one's hearers. The truth need not be the whole truth.

That goes some way toward explaining oddities connected with asserted disjunctions and conditionals. To testify to the truth of a disjunction when in a position to testify to the truth of one of its components is to deceive without actually telling a lie. Since a misleading truth can do much of the dirty work of a lie, we are tempted to call it false. But it's not.

So far as truth and falsity go, there is nothing to choose among (1) through (3); each is false in the tf case for AC, true in the other three cases:

1. C if A $A \to C$

2. C or not A $\neg A \vee C$

3. not A-but-not-C $\neg (A \wedge \neg C)$

Because (1) always agrees with (2) in truth value, oddities of "or" reappear more confusingly as oddities of "if"—more confusingly because the "if" idiom "$A \rightarrow C$" conceals a denial that the "or not" idiom "$\neg A \vee C$" puts up front. Just as "$\neg A \vee C$" follows from "C" or from "$\neg A$," so the conditional "$A \rightarrow C$" follows from its consequent or from the *denial* of its antecedent. All three of the following arguments are valid:

4. $\dfrac{C}{A \rightarrow C}$ 5. $\dfrac{\neg A}{A \rightarrow C}$ 6. $\dfrac{A}{\neg A \rightarrow C}$

Who did it? The answer "Harry, unless it was Dick" can be analyzed as a disjunction (7) or as either of the conditionals (8) or (9). Each follows from "D."

7. Harry did it or Dick did it. $H \vee D$
8. If it wasn't Harry it was Dick. $\neg H \rightarrow D$
9. If it wasn't Dick it was Harry. $\neg D \rightarrow H$

Statements 7 through 9 are logically equivalent: they all come to the same thing so far as truth and falsity are concerned, being false in the ff case for *HD* and true in the other three cases. In the mouth of one who knows that Dick did it, all are equally devious—but true.

Such ingredients of deception are recycled as zaniness in the following examples of arguments that are either interesting (on a counterfactual interpretation of "if") or valid (on a matter-of-fact interpretation) but not both.

10. *Hyperbole.* "I'll have a second cup, so I'll die before noon if I don't."

This is an argument of form "C, so if $\neg C$ then D." Its conclusion begs to be interpreted as a counterfactual because since I have already said that I will, my statement about what's true if I don't seems pointless unless it's really a claim about what *would* be true if I *didn't*. But on the counterfactual interpretation the conclusion obviously doesn't follow from the premise. Try the other interpretation. If the conclusion is interpreted as a matter-of-fact conditional "$\neg C \rightarrow D$" then the argument is valid. Being valid, it's rightly persuasive if I know that the premise is true. But persuasive of what? Of the truth of the conclusion, that $\neg C \rightarrow D$, that $C \vee D$. But of course that doesn't mean it would be fatal for me to pass up the second cup. It means only that I'll have a second cup or die before noon—which follows from "I'll have a second cup" as surely and as pointlessly as does "I'll have a second cup or fly to the moon before noon."

11. *The Consolation of Philosophy.* "I can't die before noon, for it's false that if I don't have a second cup I'll die before noon."

This is an argument of form "¬ (if ¬ *C* then *D*), so ¬ *D*". On the matter-of-fact interpretation the premise says that ¬(¬ *C* → *D*), which is true if and only if "*C*" and "*D*" are both false. From this the comforting conclusion "¬ *D*" follows; but it's no new comfort, for the premise said that and more, "¬ *C* ∧ ¬ *D*." Then on the matter-of-fact interpretation the argument is valid but pointless. Try the other. On the counterfactual interpretation the premise quite correctly denies that I'd die before noon if I didn't have a second cup; but from that denial it doesn't follow that I won't die before noon (e.g., from the strychnine in the second breakfast cup that I'm about to drink). On this interpretation the premise is true, and it would be good news if it implied the conclusion; but it doesn't.

1.13 RULES OF FORMATION

Our mother tongues aren't best adapted to display logical form clearly. Therefore people have invented a prosaic language form, logical notation, to do that. We've been using bits of it since Section 1.7. Its grammatical rules are simplicity itself. Given an initial stock of sentences (0), these rules specify five operations by which new sentences can be formed from old ones:

---

0. *Starters.* Capital letters, with or without subscripts.

1. *Denial.* Prefix "¬" to a sentence.

2. *Conjunction.* Write " ∧ " between adjacent members of a sequence of two or more sentences and enclose the result in parentheses.

3. *Disjunction.* Write " ∨ " between adjacent members of a sequence of two or more sentences and enclose the result in parentheses.

4. *Conditioning.* Write " → " between two sentences and enclose the result in parentheses.

5. *Biconditioning.* Write " ↔ " between two sentences and enclose the result in parentheses.

That's dull but clear. Notice that whatever parentheses are needed to avoid messes when new sentences are built out of old ones are provided in the rules, and in a fairly economical way. Thus, by (0), "*A*" is a sentence; by (1), so is "¬ *A*"; and by (1) again, so is "¬¬ *A*." Rule 1 doesn't make us write "¬ [¬ (*A*)]"; in fact, that's not a possible result of applying our rules. The only unnecessary parentheses that the rules mandate are the ones enclosing sentences obtained by rules 2 through 5 that don't appear as parts of longer sentences but stand alone, e.g., the parentheses in "(¬ *A* ∨ *B*)." In practice we'll omit those, writing simply "¬ *A* ∨ *B*" as we did before the rules of formation were announced. We'll always restore such missing parentheses before a sentence is compounded further.

1.14   CONSISTENCY AND THE SCIENCE OF REFUTATION

A set of sentences is consistent if there is a case in which all are true, inconsistent if there is no such case. Thus, the sentences "$A \to C$," "$A \to \neg C$," and "A" form an inconsistent set. A single sentence is said to be consistent or inconsistent (i.e., with itself) depending on whether there is or isn't a case in which it is true. Another term for inconsistent is "contradictory." An inconsistent single sentence is said to be self-contradictory, or to be a contradiction.

Clearly one can program a home computer to run truth-table tests for validity and consistency once English sentences are replaced by logical formulas—provided the number of letters isn't too large. Ten letters, 1024 cases, are manageable. A hundred letters aren't, for the number of cases would be 2^{100}, which is more than 100000 ... with 30 zeroes.* But "in principle," i.e., ignoring limitations of computation time and memory capacity, the thing can be done. And of course efficient search can push the practical limits out further.

If logic is the science of deduction, it is the science of refutation as well. From this point of view formal logic aims to provide systematic means for recognizing inconsistency. But while different features are prominent in it, this second perspective shows the same logical landscape as the first. It is straightforward to transform one point of view into the other. Here's how it goes in the truth-functional case, where it is straightforward to program computers reliably to recognize (1) sets of sentences in logical notation as consistent or inconsistent, or to recognize (2) arguments in that notation as valid or invalid—provided there aren't too many sentence letters.

How to use an inconsistency detector to test validity. Present it with the set consisting of the premises and the denial of the conclusion of the argument to be tested. If the set is inconsistent, the argument is valid; if the set is consistent, the argument is invalid.

How to use a validity detector to test inconsistency. Present it with the argument whose premises are the sentences in the set to be tested and whose conclusion is any truth-functionally inconsistent sentence, say "$C \land \neg C$." If the argument is valid, the set is inconsistent; if the argument is invalid, the set is consistent.

Thus, if the sentences in the set to be tested are those listed in (1) below, the corresponding argument will be (2).

1. $A, A \to B, A \to \neg B$ (*inconsistent*)
2. $A, A \to B, A \to \neg B, so\ C \land \neg C$ (*valid*)

---

* Because $2^{100} = (2^{10})^{10} = (1024)^{10}$, which is more than $1000^{10} = (10^3)^{10} = 10^{30}$.

The conclusion of (2) is false in all cases, but there are no counterexamples, for as the premises (1) of that argument form an inconsistent set, there is no case in which all of them are true. The inconsistency alarm will sound for a set if and only if the validity bell would ring for the corresponding argument.

1.15 TAUTOLOGIES

There are truths of reason and truths of fact, logical truths and factual truths. "Everything is identical with itself" belongs to the first category. "The earth is the third planet from the sun" to the second. Truths of fact are true in the actual case but false in one or more others; logical truths are true in all cases. Tautologies form the simplest category of logical truths: the truths of truth-functional logic, the sentences true in all cases concerning truth values of their shortest subsentences.

A **tautology** is a sentence with no f cases at all in its truth table.

Examples are "$A \lor \neg A$," "$A \rightarrow A$," "$A \lor B \lor \neg(A \land B)$."

Notice that an argument of form 1 below is truth-functionally valid if and only if the corresponding conditional 2 is a tautology:

1. Premise 1, premise 2, ..., premise n, *so* conclusion

2. (Premise 1 $\land$ premise 2 $\land$ ... $\land$ premise n) $\rightarrow$ conclusion

That's because the cases in which (2) is false are those in which its antecedent is true and its consequent false, and those are the cases in which all premises of (1) are true and its conclusion is false. It's when there are no such cases that two things happen: the argument (1) is truth-functionally valid, and the sentence (2) is a tautology.

Then truth-functional logic is the science of tautology as truly as it is the science of deduction and of refutation. Those all come to the same thing.

1.16 CONTEXT DEPENDENCY

Strictly speaking, statements are not sentences. Rather, we use sentences to make statements, as when I utter the sentence "Father knew Lloyd George" to tell Lavinia (falsely, in fact) that M. M. Jeffrey knew the prime minister. But not every occasion on which a declarative sentence is uttered or written or tapped out in Morse code is an occasion on which a statement is thereby made; the sentence might have been uttered as part of a song, or written to practice calligraphy, or tapped out to test the circuit. Nor are sentences the only vehicles for statement making; in suitable circumstances a shrug or a nod or a silence will do the job.

It often happens that the same declarative sentence can be used to make one statement or another depending on who utters it, when and where it is uttered, to whom it is addressed, and with what accompanying gestures or conversational context. "I saw you chatting with him here yesterday" is a case in point. The conversational context determines the referent of "him" if that sentence was a reply to Min's claim that she hadn't seen Henry Crun in years, but the nonconversational context (e.g., place and time of utterance) can be equally important in determining what statement, if any, the speaker or writer or telegrapher makes by a particular act of speech, writing, or telegraphy.

Difficulties about context dependency are at a minimum in scientific and mathematical discourse. If we were concerned only with statements like "Whales are mammals" and "There are infinitely many prime numbers," we could ignore the fact that it's people, not sentences, who make statements, for (nearly enough) anyone, anywhere, any time who utters such a sentence thereby makes the same statement that anyone else would, anywhere, any time by uttering that sentence. But except in such carefully controlled circumstances, context dependency is as pervasive as the air we breathe, and as unobtrusive. It doesn't cross our minds that two people might be contradicting each other when one says "I went to Grantchester yesterday" and the other replies "I didn't," nor are we tempted to symbolize the second statement by "$\neg A$" once we have used "A" for the first.

But when in logic we formulate general truths about validity, inconsistency, etc., it's a help to be able to depend on all the sentences we meet being context-independent. To arrange that, we imagine that English has been replaced by a well-behaved artificial language called "Logic" with a capital "L." (Less fancifully: we use logical notation in place of English.) In Logic we eliminate context dependency by fixing the truth values of sentence letters so as to leave them unaffected by subsequent contexts of use. Thus, in the exchange about Grantchester we interpret "A" as a context-independent sentence which, uttered by anyone, anywhere, any time, in conditions suitable for statement making, produces a statement that can be depended on to have the same truth value as the statement that the first speaker made by saying "I went to Grantchester yesterday." This sort of thing:

Black: "You won't take that knight and win." $\neg(K \wedge W)$
White: "You think not? Here goes." K
Black: "That does it. You've blown the game." $So \neg W$

In logical notation the second premise, "K," is interpreted as having the same truth value as White's statement, whichever that may be, and similarly, in the conclusion, the statement letter "W" is assigned a truth value (t or f, as may be) opposite to that of Black's final statement. Given those assignments, "$\neg(K \wedge W)$" is a context-independent vehicle for making a statement that has the same truth value as Black's opening challenge. You can do all that without understanding chess.

For the most part, logical notation is parasitic upon ordinary talk in such ways as we have just seen. Truth values of sentence letters are fixed (until further notice) in relation to the truth values of certain actual statements. But we need not know those statements' truth values when we make those stipulations, or, indeed, ever. Similarly the khan's subjects can promise him his weight in gold without being able to put a number to it either when they make the promise or when they keep it by loading gold onto one pan of a balance until the khan, on the other, rises just clear of the ground.

1.17 FORMAL VALIDITY

Truth-functional validity of the argument from "Sharks are mammals" (B) to "Whales or sharks are mammals" ($A \vee B$) was explained as absence of cases where "B" is true (sharks are mammals) but "$A \vee B$" is false (whales or sharks aren't). But that wasn't meant to be just because there are no cases at all in which sharks are mammals, for if there are no such cases, then there are no counterexamples to the argument from "Sharks are mammals" to any conclusion you please, e.g., the conclusion that the world came to an end in the year 1000. If we don't want to count all those arguments as truth-functionally valid, we'll have to define "case" more clearly.

What would a case be, in which sharks are mammals? Are we meant to imagine an alternative course of evolution, rather like the actual one except that in it the line of development that led to today's sharks led to some species of mammals? (What mammals? Wolves? Gerbils? Perhaps mammals that don't exist in our world?) Should questions of logic depend on which real or imaginary mammals count as "sharks" in our search for counterexamples? Is it an arbitrary terminological matter? If so, why not just say that nonactual cases are extraordinary interpretations of ordinary terms?

Changes from the actual case to others won't then be changes from the actual world to other possible worlds, but only changes in our interpretation of terms—i.e., in truth-functional logic, of sentence letters. Our interpretation of "A" and "B" as, say, "Whales are mammals" and "Sharks are mammals" bears on the soundness of the argument from "B" to "$A \vee B$" but not on its validity. That interpretation's bearing on soundness consists entirely in its determination of the tf case for AB (case 2 in Section 1.5) as actual. But the question of validity is independent of that determination. Validity concerns all four cases that arise when "A" and "B" are interpreted so as to make both true (case 1), one true and one false (cases 2 and 3), or both false (case 4). So long as the truth values are tt, tf, ft, and ff in the four cases, the four interpretations that give "*A*" and "*B*" those truth values can be anything we please. In truth-functional logic further particulars can't matter because here truth values of premise and conclusion depend only on truth values of the letters, not on how the letters get those truth values. Case 1 might be defined as the one in which "*A*" has the same truth value as "Apples are not antelopes" and "*B*" has the same truth value as "Benjamin Franklin invented bifocal eyeglasses," but since such particulars can't matter, we may as well go for certainty and simplicity, perhaps using "$0 = 0$" as an all-purpose truth and "$0 = 1$" as an all-purpose falsehood. And since it really doesn't matter, there's no need to settle on any one such interpretation; hence the bare "t"s and "f"s in the truth table. It's only when we inquire into the identity of the actual case that we need to know the actual interpretations of terms.

To establish truth-functional validity of any one argument of form "*B*, so $A \lor B$" is to establish validity of all arguments of that form. Validity of any argument is a matter of form, not interpretation. That's why it's *formal* logic that's the science of deduction.

1.18 PROBLEMS

For most of the following problems partial solutions are provided at the back of the book.

1. Interpret "*E*," "*J*," and "*M*" as meaning that the earth is the third planet from the sun, that Jupiter is, and that Mars is, and work out the truth values of the following sentences (i.e., their real truth values, in the actual case).
   (a) $(M \land J) \lor E$ (b) $M \land (J \lor E)$
   (c) $\neg(M \lor J \lor E)$ (d) $\neg M \lor J \lor E$
   (e) $\neg(\neg M \lor \neg J \lor \neg E)$ (f) $\neg(\neg M \land \neg J \land \neg E)$

2. "Thin is guilty," observed Watson, "because (i) either Holmes is right and the vile Moriarty is guilty or he is wrong and the scurrilous Thin did the job; but (ii) those scoundrels are either both guilty or both innocent; and, as usual, (iii) Holmes is right." (a) Is the argument valid? (b) Is the conclusion consistent with the premises? Use "*T, M*" for "Thin is guilty, Moriarty is guilty," "$\neg T, \neg M$" for innocence, "*H*" for "Holmes is right." Do these first efficiently, then by truth tables.

3. *Dilemma.* Show that this argument is valid: $A \lor B$, $A \to C$, $B \to C$, so *C*. Do this first efficiently, then by truth tables.

4. *Syllogism.* And this: $A_1 \to A_2$, $A_2 \to A_3$, ..., $A_{99} \to A_{100}$; so $A_1 \to A_{100}$. (In a counterexample the conclusion is false. That gives you truth values of two letters. Is it possible for all premises to be true, given those two?)

5. Which of these is a tautology? Do these first efficiently, then by truth tables.
   (a) Either Min is home or she and Hen are not both home, $A \lor \neg(A \land C)$.
   (b) Either Min is home or she and Hen are both not home, $A \lor (\neg A \land \neg C)$.

6. Symbolize the following in the notation of Section 1.3; find counterexamples, if any.

(a) Moriarty: "If Min is home, so is Henry." Thin: "Indeed; and if Min is home, Henry isn't." Moriarty: "Ah, I see: Min's not home!"

(b) "Min's home if Henry is, but he isn't, so she isn't."

(c) "It's false that if Min is home, she's on board. Then if she's home, she's not on board."

(d) "It's false that if Min is home, she's on board, because if she's home, she's not on board."

(e) "Look, we know that Min is on board if Henry is home. Then she has to be on board if she's home, because Henry's home if she is." ("Then" flags the conclusion.)

7. True or false? Justify your answer by an argument or counterexample, as appropriate.

(a) If a sentence is not a logical truth, its denial must be one.

(b) If a sentence is not consistent, its denial must be a logical truth.

(c) If a sentence doesn't follow from another, its denial must.

(d) If a sentence doesn't follow from another, its denial can't.

(e) If a set of sentences is consistent, each member must be.

(f) If each member is consistent, so must be the set.

(g) You can't make a valid argument invalid by adding premises.

(h) You can't make an invalid argument valid by removing premises.

8. *Exclusive disjunction, equivalence.* Use the symbol " $\underline{\vee}$ " for "or" in the exclusive sense. The exclusive disjunction " $A \underline{\vee} B$ " is true when " A " and " B " disagree in truth value, false when they agree. Construct a common truth table for the following. Which are logically equivalent?

(a) $A \underline{\vee} B$ (b) $\neg(A \leftrightarrow B)$ (c) $A \leftrightarrow \neg B$ (d) $\neg A \leftrightarrow B$

9. "Neither A nor B" is an idiomatic way of denying "either A or B," and it's also an idiomatic way of asserting "not A and not B." What does that say about the view that the basic use of "or" in English is exclusive?

10. "*Tom, Dick, or Harry.*" If the answer "Tom, Dick, or Harry" (ungrouped "$A \underline{\vee} B \underline{\vee} C$") to the question "Who did it?" means *just one of them*, then "$A \underline{\vee} B \underline{\vee} C$" isn't logically equivalent to "$(A \underline{\vee} B) \underline{\vee} C$"—which *is* logically equivalent to "$A \underline{\vee} (B \underline{\vee} C)$."

(a) Work out the truth tables for those three, and see why.

(b) Give a concise verbal rule of valuation for "$(A \underline{\vee} B) \underline{\vee} C$."

(c) What does all this say about "or" in English?

11. *More astounding arguments.* Diagnose the following, as was done in Section 1.12:

(a) *True grit.* "I'll ski tomorrow. Then I'll ski tomorrow if I break my leg today."

(b) *Perils of foresight.* "I'll break my leg today. I know that because I know it's false that if I break my leg today I'll ski tomorrow."

(c) *Premise bonanza!* Knowing that Dr. Adams or Dr. Brown will operate, and learning that Dr. Brown won't, you conclude that if Dr. Adams doesn't operate, Dr. Brown will.

(d) *Zapping them with logic.* "We'll win, for if they withdraw if we advance, we'll win, and we won't advance!"

12. *Probability.* The probability that a sentence is true is the sum of the probabil-

ities of its t cases, and is zero if it has none. Find the probabilities of sentences *a* through *e* on the assumption that the probabilities of the cases tt, tf, ft, ff for *AC* are .1, .2, .3, .4, respectively.

(*a*) $\neg A \vee C$ (*b*) $\neg(A \vee C)$ (*c*) $\neg A \vee \neg C$
(*d*) $\neg(A \wedge C)$ (*e*) $A \leftrightarrow C$

13. *Conditional probability.* The conditional probability of one sentence given a second is the ratio of the probability that they are both true to the probability that the second is. With "*A*" and "*C*" meaning that Min is home and that Henry is home, and with probabilities of the cases as in (12), find the conditional probability that:
(*a*) Min is home, given that Henry is.
(*b*) Henry is home, given that Min is.
(*c*) Both are home, given that at least one is.
(*d*) Both are home, given that exactly one is.
(*e*) Exactly one is home, given that at least one is.

14. *More probability.* Probabilities of cases tt, tf, ft, ff for *TN* are *p, q, r, s*. Suppose the probability of rain tomorrow and the next day $(T \wedge N)$ is the same as the probability of rain tomorrow *or* the next day $(T \vee N)$. What is then the probability of the same weather on both days $(T \leftrightarrow N)$?

15. *Knights and knaves.* Knaves always lie, knights always tell the truth, and in Transylvania, where everybody is one or the other (but you can't tell which by looking), you encounter two people, one of whom says "He's a knight or I'm a knave." What are they?*

16. *Cretans.* "One of themselves, even a prophet of their own, said: The Cretans are always liars, evil beasts, slow bellies." So Paul says, adding "This witness is true." Is *that* true?†

---

* Thanks to Raymond Smullyan, *What is the Name of This Book?* Prentice-Hall, Englewood Cliffs, N.J., 1978.
† Thanks to Paul of Tarsus, Epistle to Titus, I, 12.

2

TRUTH TREES

We have seen that validity of an argument comes to the same thing as inconsistency of the set consisting of its premises and the denial of its conclusion, i.e., nonexistence of counterexamples, cases where all members of that set are true. Thus, validity of the argument

$$B \to \neg A$$
$$\neg B \to C$$
$$\overline{A \to C}$$

comes to the same thing as inconsistency of the set consisting of the sentences

1     $B \to \neg A$ (premise)
2     $\neg B \to C$ (premise)
3     $\neg(A \to C)$ ($\neg$ conclusion)

The straightforward, inefficient method of verifying inconsistency has us calculate the truth values of 1, 2, 3 in the eight cases ttt, ttf, fft, tff, ftt, ftf, fft, fff regarding ABC to see whether or not 1, 2, 3 are all t in any cases. If so, the set is consistent, the argument invalid; if not, the set is inconsistent, the argument valid. The more efficient approach that was repeatedly illustrated in Chapter 1 greatly reduced the labor by examining whole blocks of cases at once. The method of truth trees that will now be explained routinizes that approach just as the method of truth tables routinizes the straightforward, inefficient approach. In the present example, with only three sentence letters, the tree method only decreases the drudgery, but with a dozen sentence letters or a hundred the tree method can cut the size of validity tests down from the impossible to what we can deal with by hand or machine. The argument shown above provides an example.

2.1   A CLOSED TREE

The argument is valid, the set inconsistent. That's shown by the fact that the completed tree (at the end of this section) is closed, i.e., in each path through it, top to bottom, some sentence and its denial both appear as full lines. Let's see how we get there.

Start.   The tree starts with sentences 1, 2, 3 as above. Are there any cases in which all of those are true?

Step 1.   We begin with sentence 3 because there's only one case in which it is true; the denial of a conditional is true iff the conditional itself is false, i.e., its antecedent is true and its consequent false. So we write "A" and "$\neg C$" as new lines 4, 5, and we check ($\checkmark$) line 3 to indicate that we are done with it. It is exactly in the case in which line 3 is true that the two new lines are both true; that's why line 3 can now be ignored. The move from line 3 to lines 4 and 5 is summed up by the *rule of inference* for denied conditionals $\neg(\bigcirc \to \triangle)$ shown at the right, where the circle and triangle stand for arbitrary sentences.

1	$B \to \neg A$	(premise)	
2	$\neg B \to C$	(premise)	
3	$\checkmark \neg(A \to C)$	($\neg$ conclusion)	$\checkmark \neg(\bigcirc \to \triangle)$
4	A	(from 3)	$\bigcirc$
5	$\neg C$	(from 3)	$\neg \triangle$

Step 2.   We check line 1 next. (Line 2 would have done as well.) The three cases in which line 1 is true fall into two overlapping categories: those in which its antecedent "B" is false, and those in which its consequent "$\neg A$" is true. Then at line 5 the trunk of the upside-down tree divides into two branches, starting with the left- and right-hand entries in line 6. The move from line 1 to line 6 is summed up by the rule of inference for conditionals $\bigcirc \to \triangle$ shown at the right.

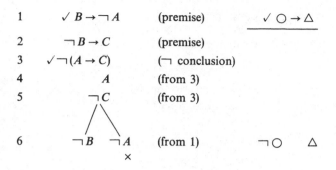

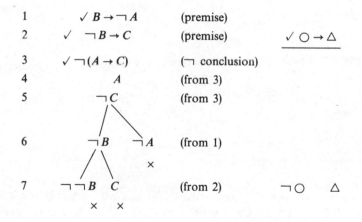

But the right-hand path is closed: it contains a sentence and its denial as full lines 4, 6. The attempt that path represents, to find cases in which 1, 2, 3 are all true, is a failure. We show that by putting an ex (×) at the bottom of the path.

Step 3. Finally, we apply the rule of inference for conditionals to line 2, splitting the still-open path at line 6 into two stubby branches with the entries in line 7. (At line 6 the closed right-hand branch is dead; it can grow no more.) At line 2 the conditional $\bigcirc \to \triangle$ is "$\neg B \to C$," and so the circle stands for "$\neg B$" and the circle preceded by "$\neg$" stands for "$\neg \neg B$" in line 7.

The exes at the bottoms of the two new branches indicate that they are closed: the left-hand one contains a sentence "$\neg B$" and its denial "$\neg \neg B$" as full lines 6, 7, and the other contains "C" and "$\neg C$" as full lines 7, 5.

The tree is finished. All attempts to find cases in which all the sentences we started with are true have failed: the set $\{1, 2, 3\}$ is inconsistent, the argument from 1 and 2 to the conclusion denied by 3 is valid.

2.2 AN OPEN FINISHED TREE

In contrast, see what happens when we test an invalid argument, e.g.,

$$A \to B, \neg A, \text{ so } B$$

The tree starts with the premises and the denial of the conclusion, and grows just one more level, when we check line 1.

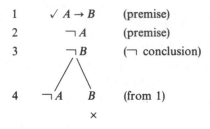

The open path represents a counterexample, a case in which 1, 2, 3 are all true. That is the case in which the unchecked sentences "$\neg A$" and "$\neg B$" in the path are true, the ff case for AB. There the premises are true, the conclusion, "B," false.

2.3 DOUBLE DENIAL

The tree test for validity of the valid argument

$$\frac{A}{\neg\neg A}$$

begins as follows:

1   A (premise)
2    $\neg\neg\neg A$ ($\neg$ conclusion)

So far, the tree remains open; its one path does not contain a sentence and its denial as full lines. To close it we need another rule of inference: erase initial double denials, "$\neg\ \neg$." This allows us to add a third line, and close the tree. The new rule of inference is shown at the right.

1   A (premise)
2   $\checkmark \neg\neg\neg A$ ($\neg$ conclusion) $\checkmark \underline{\neg\neg\bigcirc}$
3      $\neg A$ (from 2) $\bigcirc$
        ×

2.4 FLOWCHART FOR "¬" AND "→," WITH EXAMPLES

The procedure for constructing these truth trees is summarized in the flow-chart of Figure 2.1; it can be applied with pencil and paper, or programmed as computer software. What isn't included in the flowchart is advice about

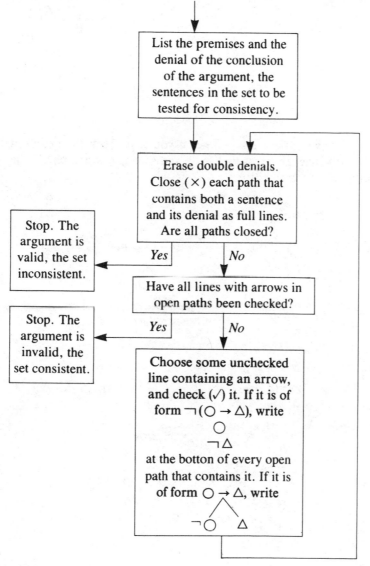

FIGURE 2.1
Flowchart for trees with "¬" and "→."

the order in which to check lines in order to make the test end as fast as possible: "Other things equal, check denied conditionals before undenied ones as a way of minimizing bushiness of the tree."

Try the tree method on the following arguments. You will get one tree or another (but the same answer—valid or invalid) depending on the order in which you choose to check lines.

(a) A (b) B (c) $\neg A$

$\dfrac{A \to B}{B}$ $\dfrac{A \to B}{A}$ $\dfrac{}{A \to B}$

(d) $A \to B$ (e) $\neg A \to B$ (f) $A \to B$

$\dfrac{B \to C}{A \to C}$ $\dfrac{}{B \to A}$ $\dfrac{}{\neg B \to \neg A}$

Solutions follow, showing the trees you get if you first check the denial of the conclusion if it's checkable (has an "$\to$"), and then check any checkable premises in order, from top to bottom.

Solutions

(a) A (b) B (c) $\neg A$

(d) $\checkmark A \to B$ (e) $\checkmark \neg A \to B$ (f) $\checkmark A \to B$

Notice that if even one path is open after all formulas containing arrows have been checked, the argument is invalid, for each open path represents a class of counterexamples. Thus, in example e the right-hand path represents a class of counterexamples consisting of all cases in which "A" is false and "B" is true. Now try these, for which you'll find solutions at the end of the book.

(g) $\dfrac{(A \to B) \to C}{\neg C \to A}$ (h) $\dfrac{(A \to B) \to A}{A}$

(i) $\dfrac{(A \to B) \to B}{A}$ (j) $A \to B$

$\dfrac{}{}$ $B \to C$

$\dfrac{C \to D}{A \to D}$

(k) Moriarty will escape unless Holmes acts ($\neg H \to M$). We rely on Watson only if Holmes does not act ($W \to \neg H$). So if Holmes does not act, Moriarty will escape unless we rely on Watson.

2.5 RULES OF INFERENCE, WITH FLOW CHART

So far our method applies only to arguments in which "$\neg$" and "$\to$" are the only connectives, but we can easily extend it to other truth-functional connectives by providing more rules of inference. The array in Table 2.1 shows a pair of rules of inference for each of the five truth-functional connectives for which we have adopted special symbols in logical notation.

   The first of these may be thought of as an inference from two premises—one the denial of the other—to the conclusion "$\times$" that, as the premises contradict each other, the path in which they occur as full lines determines no counterexamples. All the other rules have a single premise, the assertion (upper rules) or denial (lower) of a sentence in which one of "$\neg$," "$\to$," "$\wedge$," "$\vee$," "$\leftrightarrow$" is the main connective.

TABLE 2.1
Rules of inference

$\bigcirc$	$\checkmark\,(\bigcirc \to \triangle)$	$\checkmark\,(\bigcirc \wedge \triangle)$	$\checkmark\,(\bigcirc \vee \triangle)$	$\checkmark\,(\bigcirc \leftrightarrow \triangle)$
$\dfrac{\neg\bigcirc}{\times}$	$\dfrac{}{\neg\bigcirc \quad \triangle}$	$\dfrac{}{\bigcirc}$ $\triangle$	$\dfrac{}{\bigcirc \quad \triangle}$	$\dfrac{}{\bigcirc \quad \neg\bigcirc}$ $\triangle \quad \neg\triangle$
$\checkmark\,\neg\neg\bigcirc$	$\checkmark\,\neg(\bigcirc \to \triangle)$	$\checkmark\,\neg(\bigcirc \wedge \triangle)$	$\checkmark\,\neg(\bigcirc \vee \triangle)$	$\checkmark\,\neg(\bigcirc \leftrightarrow \triangle)$
$\dfrac{}{\bigcirc}$	$\dfrac{}{\bigcirc}$ $\neg\triangle$	$\dfrac{}{\neg\bigcirc \quad \neg\triangle}$	$\dfrac{}{\neg\bigcirc}$ $\neg\triangle$	$\dfrac{}{\neg\bigcirc \quad \bigcirc}$ $\triangle \quad \neg\triangle$

Any one of these rules can be applied to any unchecked sentence of the form indicated in the first line of the rule, where it appears as a full line of an open path. Thus, the rule in the middle of the second row can be applied to the sentence "$\neg((A \rightarrow B) \wedge (\neg A \wedge B))$" where it appears as a full line of a path, because that sentence is a denied conjunction, $\neg(\bigcirc \wedge \triangle)$, with "$(A \rightarrow B)$" in place of the circle and "$(\neg A \wedge B)$" in place of the triangle. No other rule applies to that sentence, for it has form $\neg(\bigcirc \wedge \triangle)$ and no other. It is true that parts of that sentence have other forms: the $\bigcirc$ part "$(A \rightarrow B)$" is a conditional, the $\triangle$ part "$(\neg A \wedge B)$" is an undenied conjunction, and so is the part of the full sentence that remains when the shell "$\neg(\ )$" is stripped away. But the rules of inference are only to be applied to sentences that appear as full lines of open paths, not to their subsentences.

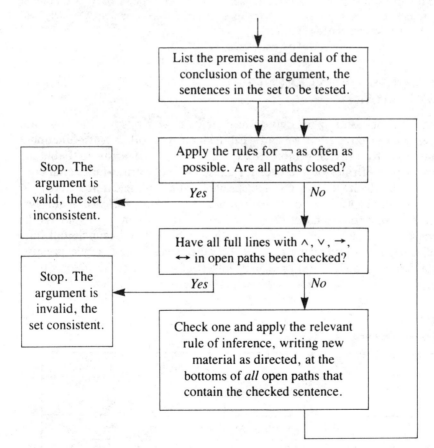

FIGURE 2.2
Flowchart for rules of inference.

The program for applying the rules of inference is essentially the same as it was when we had only the rules for $\neg$ and $\rightarrow$ (see Figure 2.2). The rules may be applied in any order, but usually it is best to begin with ones that involve no branching: the lower rules for $\rightarrow$ and $\vee$ and the upper rule for $\wedge$, if there are any lines to which these apply.

For simplicity, the rules for $\wedge$ and $\vee$ have been given for two-component conjunctions and disjunctions, but the rules are similar when there are more components. Thus, for three components, the rules are as shown in Table 2.2.

TABLE 2.2

Rules of inference for triple conjunctions and disjunctions

$\checkmark$ (O $\wedge$ $\triangle$ $\wedge$ $\square$)	$\checkmark$ (O $\vee$ $\triangle$ $\vee$ $\square$)
O $\triangle$ $\square$	O $\quad$ $\triangle$ $\quad$ $\square$
$\checkmark$ $\neg$(O $\wedge$ $\triangle$ $\wedge$ $\square$)	$\checkmark$ $\neg$(O $\vee$ $\triangle$ $\vee$ $\square$)
$\neg$O $\quad$ $\neg\triangle$ $\quad$ $\neg\square$	$\neg$O $\neg\triangle$ $\neg\square$

There are no such three-component rules for $\rightarrow$ or $\leftrightarrow$, because expressions like "$A \rightarrow B \rightarrow C$" and "$A \leftrightarrow B \leftrightarrow C$" do not count as sentences.

Now try these. (There are solutions at the back of the book.)

(*l*) $A \leftrightarrow B$, so $A \rightarrow B$

(*m*) $A \rightarrow B$, so $A \leftrightarrow B$

(*n*) $A \wedge B$, so $A \vee B$

2.6 PROBLEMS

1. Apply the tree test to the arguments in Sections 1.1, 1.3, 1.4, and 1.6 (of Chap. 1), to arguments (4), (5), and (6) in Section 1.12, and to the set (1) and the argument (2) in Section 1.14.

2. Use the tree method.
   (*a*) If Holmes has bungled (*A*) or Watson's on the job (*B*), then Moriarty will escape (*C*). Does it follow that Moriarty will escape unless Holmes bungles?
   (*b*) Moriarty will escape only if Holmes bungles. Holmes will not bungle if Watson's to be believed (*B*). Does it follow that if Watson's to be believed, Moriarty will not escape?

(c) If Moriarty has escaped, then either Holmes has bungled or Watson's on the job. Holmes has not bungled unless Moriarty has escaped. Watson's not on the job. Does it follow that Moriarty has escaped if and only if Holmes has bungled?

(d) Moriarty will not escape unless Holmes acts (A). We shall rely on Watson (B) only if Holmes does not act. Does it follow that if Holmes does not act, Moriarty will escape unless we rely on Watson?

(e) $(A \land B) \to C, \neg A \to D$, so $B \to (C \lor D)$.

3. Test the consistency of these sets of sentences by the tree method. (These aren't arguments. Each tree starts with a list of the members of the set, undenied. The set is consistent iff there is at least one open path through the finished tree.)

(a) $A, \neg A$

(b) $A \to B, A \to \neg B$

(c) $B \to A, B \to \neg A$

(d) Both Thin and Moriarty are guilty if either is.
If neither is guilty then Holmes has not bungled.
Unless Holmes has bungled, exactly one of them is guilty.

4. *Tautology.* To see whether or not a sentence is a tautology, start a tree with its denial and proceed as if you were testing an argument for validity. If the tree closes, the sentence is a tautology, and if not, not. Test these:

(a) $A \to A$

(b) $A \to (\neg A \to A)$

(c) $(A \to \neg A) \to A$

(d) $[A \to (B \to C)] \to [(A \to B) \to (A \to \neg B)]$

5. *A common misconception.* It may seem plausible that we can tell whether or not a sentence is a tautology by starting a tree with the sentence itself, *undenied*, and concluding that the sentence is a tautology iff every path in the finished tree is *open*. Try this method on the following two sentences, and notice that it gives the wrong answers.

(a) A (b) $A \lor \neg A \lor (A \land \neg A)$

(c) Does this bogus test always give incorrect answers?

6. *Logical equivalence = mutual implication.* $\bigcirc$ and $\triangle$ are logically equivalent if and only if $\triangle$ follows from $\bigcirc$ and vice versa, i.e., iff "$\triangle$, so $\bigcirc$" and "$\bigcirc$, so $\triangle$" are both valid arguments.

(a) Explain why.

(b) Using two trees, demonstrate that "$\neg(A \lor B)$" is logically equivalent to "$(\neg A \land \neg B)$."

7. (a) Formulate rules of inference in the style of Section 2.5 for exclusive disjunctions ($\bigcirc \veebar \triangle$) and their denials $\neg(\bigcirc \veebar \triangle)$.

(b) Demonstrate by the tree method that the following are not logically equivalent:

$$\neg(A \veebar B) \qquad (\neg A \land \neg B)$$

8. By the tree method, test the following three-membered set of sentences for consistency. "If Paul lives in Paris, he lives in France. It's false that if Paul lives in

London, he lives in France. It's false that if Paul lives in Paris he lives in England."*

9. "If Adams wins the election, Brown will retire to private life. If Brown dies before the election, Adams will win it. Therefore, if Brown dies before the election, he will retire to private life." Translate into logical notation, using the arrow for "if ... then," and test validity by the tree method. (More evidence that English conditionals aren't truth-functional?†)

10. Is this argument sound? If not, why not? "This argument is unsound, for its conclusion is false, and it is unsound if it has a false conclusion."

2.7 ADEQUACY OF THE TREE TEST

Figure 2.2 represents the tree test as a program applicable to an initial list of sentences, the members of a set to be tested for consistency. The tree test is adequate if (a) it always terminates, correctly classifying the initial list either as (b) inconsistent (c) or consistent. If the initial list consisted of the premises and denial of the conclusion of an argument, (b) means that the argument was valid and (c) means that it was invalid. We now prove that the tree test is adequate in those three respects.

a. Assuming that the initial list doesn't go on forever, the test does eventually terminate. That's called "decidability": the test can be relied on eventually to decide about consistency of the initial list (and about validity of the corresponding argument, if that's how the list originated). But there remain questions about correctness of that decision.

b. If the decision was "inconsistent" (or "valid"), we can trust it. That's *soundness* of the test—a different thing from soundness of an argument, which means validity with all premises true. Soundness of the tree test means that it never calls a consistent set inconsistent or an invalid argument valid: see Figure 2.3.

c. If the decision was "consistent" (or "invalid"), we can trust it. That's *completeness* of the tree test for inconsistency and validity. To say the same thing the other way around: completeness means that whenever the initial list really is inconsistent, the test will say so: see Figure 2.3.

The tree test is sound and complete because the one-premise rules of inference were designed to have certain properties that are crucial for

---

* It has been argued that the result of that test is bad news for the view that English conditionals are truth-functional: see Brian Ellis, *Rational Belief Systems*, Blackwell, Oxford, Eng. 1979, p. 61.

† Ernest W. Adams, *The Logic of Conditionals*, D. Reidel, Dordrecht, Neth., 1975.

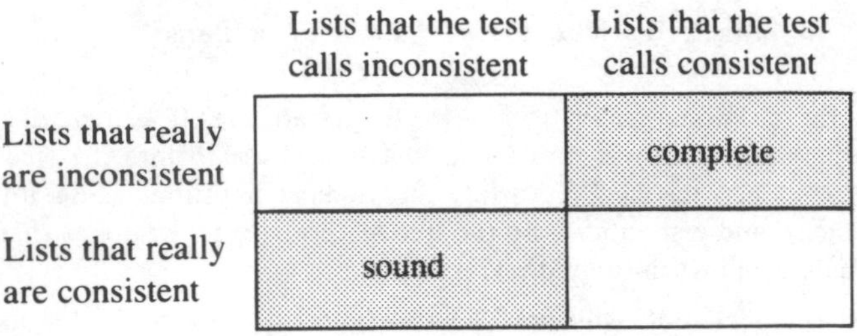

	Lists that the test calls inconsistent	Lists that the test calls consistent
Lists that really are inconsistent		complete
Lists that really are consistent	sound	

FIGURE 2.3
Soundness and completeness: shaded regions are empty.

soundness and completeness—properties to which we also apply those names.

> For a one-premise rule of inference, **soundness** means that if the premise is true in a case, all lines in its list of conclusions (or in one of its lists of conclusions) are true in that case, and **completeness** means that if all lines in a list of conclusions are true in a case, then the premise is true in that case.

Example. The line is "$(A \leftrightarrow B)$" as in Section 2.5 (l), and the case is ff for AB. The line is true in this case, and by soundness of the rule for $(\bigcirc \leftrightarrow \triangle)$ so are both lines in one list of conclusions, i.e., lines "$\neg A$" and "$\neg B$" in the right-hand list. Completeness says that since both right-hand conclusions are true in this ff case, so is the premise "$(A \leftrightarrow B)$."

2.8 DECIDABILITY

The program of Figure 2.2 must terminate in one of the two "Stop" boxes at the left after some finite number of passes through the "Check one" box at the bottom—maybe, 0 passes. Reasons: (1) the tree begins with a finite number of sentences, each of finite length (counting letters, connectives, and parentheses), and (2) the tree grows by a process of choosing an unchecked line of an open path, checking it, and adding to the tree some finite number of lines, each of which is *shorter* than the line checked. (In Section 2.5 the conclusions of the one-premise rules are 2, 3, or 4 lines shorter than their premises.) Eventually a point must be reached where all unchecked sentences in open paths have length 1 (letters) or 2 (denials of letters), whereupon the process ends with a positive answer to one of the questions asked in the middle boxes; there's no way to go endlessly round the loop in Figure 2.2.

Now let's spell that out in a proof of decidability.

> **Decidability** of the tree test means that if the initial list is finite, the test terminates after some finite number of steps.

In terms of the program, a step can be identified as a passage through the bottom box, checking a line of the tree and applying the relevant one-premise rule of inference.

Example. If the checked line is "$(A \leftrightarrow B)$," each open path in which it appears is split into two longer paths by adding lines "A" and "B" at the left and "$\neg A$" and "$\neg B$" at the right. The unchecked lines of length 5 decrease by 1, those of lengths 1 and 2 increase.

Proof. Define a tree's census as a sequence of numbers: first, the number of unchecked lines of length 1 in the tree; second, the number of unchecked lines of length 2; and so on and on, without end. If the tree has only a finite number of lines, all these numbers after a certain point will be 0, and at each passage through the bottom box, checking a line and adding new lines, the census gets smaller in this sense: at the rightmost position where they differ (as they will), the new census has a smaller entry than the old. Now with "smaller census" so defined, every sequence of smaller and smaller censuses must come to an end after some finite number of steps,* at which point we reach a "stop" arrow.

2.9 SOUNDNESS

Soundness of the tree test means that in Figure 2.2 the upper "stop" arrow is correctly annotated: if there are no open paths through the finished tree, the initial list is inconsistent. Or we can put the same matter the other way around, as follows:

> **Soundness** of the tree test means that if the initial list is consistent, there will be an open path through any tree obtainable from it by the rules of inference.

(These trees needn't be finished. And we mean the initial list itself to be counted as such a tree; certainly, if it is consistent, none of its lines are denials of others.)

---

* Because "descending chains" are always finite: starting from any census you can go up to larger and larger censuses without end, but if each step descends to a smaller census, you'll eventually come to an end with the null census, an unending sequence of zeros.

Proof. Suppose that in some case (call it "*C*") each full line of the initial list is true. Then the initial list must be open, for if it contained both a sentence and its denial as full lines, then since denial reverses truth values (Section 1.11), one of those lines would be false in *C*. And because all our rules of inference are sound, we know that when all lines of a full path are true in *C* and a rule of inference is applied to one of its lines, the new line or lines in at least one of the path's extensions are also true in *C*. Then when the tree finally stops growing, it will contain a full path in which all lines are true in *C*. Like the initial list (and for the same reason) that path must be open.

2.10 COMPLETENESS

Completeness of the tree test means that in Figure 2.2 the lower "stop" arrow is correctly annotated.

Completeness of the tree test means that if there is even one open path through a finished tree, the initial list is consistent.

Proof. Suppose that a finished tree contains some open path *P*. Now consider the case *C* in which sentence letters appearing as full lines of *P* are true and all other sentence letters in lines of *P* are false. In particular, letters whose denials appear as full lines are false because those denials are true in *C*. To show that the initial list is consistent, we show that all lines of *P* are true in *C*. (Then indeed all lines of the initial list are true in some case.)

The tree is finished, so if a rule of inference is applicable to a line of *P*, then some list of conclusions obtainable from that line by that rule is in *P*. As the rules of inference are complete, truth in *C* will be drawn upward from lines already known to be true in *C* to the longer lines from which they came via rules of inference. This drawing-up process is complete after a finite number of steps—one step for each "√" in path *P*. Thus all full lines of *P* (including all full lines in the initial list) are true in *C*.

3

GENERALITY

So far our analyses of sentences have stopped at atoms that are themselves sentences. For example:

If Watson can trap Moriarty, Holmes can. $(W \rightarrow H)$
Holmes can't. $\neg H$
_____
Watson can't. $\neg W$

Here premises and conclusion are molecules constructed out of atomic sentences by truth-functional connectives. Logical forms of premises and conclusion are displayed by using sentence letters as atoms of the analysis and using parentheses, denial signs, and arrows to form molecules out of atoms. Formal validity of such arguments is validity in virtue of the molecular structure of premises and conclusions, ignoring the structure of atoms. But much of our reasoning defies analysis in such terms. Example:

Holmes, if anyone, can trap Moriarty.
Holmes can't.
_____
No one can.

To show that this argument is valid we carry the analysis on below the atomic level, analyzing sentences into parts that are not themselves sentences or truth-functional connectives. To begin, we restate premises and conclusion in a mixture of English and the logical notation already at our disposal, to bring logical structure into view:

For all x (x can trap Moriarty → Holmes can trap Moriarty)
¬ Holmes can trap Moriarty.
_____

¬ For some x, x can trap Moriarty.

We need new logical notation for the quantifying phrases in the first premise and the conclusion:

>*Universal quantifier*, "for all x": $\forall x$
>
>*Existential quantifier*, "for some x": $\exists x$

Using small letters "a," "b" as names of Holmes and Moriarty, and the capital letter "T" for the relational phrase "can trap," we now write the argument in full logical notation, where "Tab" is an atomic sentence.

$\forall x(Txb \rightarrow Tab)$	Holmes, if anyone, can trap Moriarty.
¬ Tab	Holmes can't.
_____	_____
¬$\exists x\ Txb$	No one can.

In high school algebra variables always stand for numbers, but elsewhere in mathematics, and in logic, they can stand for things of all sorts. In any particular argument, the set of things that a variable can stand for is called the *domain* of that variable.

Showing that this argument is valid is a matter of showing that its premises and the denial of its conclusion cannot all be true, regardless of what things make up the domain of values of the variable "x," regardless of what members of that domain are named by "a" and "b," and regardless of how we interpret "T" as a relation between members of that domain.

Now let us see how the tree can be extended to test validity of this argument. As in Chapter 2 we list the premises and denial of the conclusion, and apply the rule for double denial:

1	$\forall x(Txb \rightarrow Tab)$	(premise)
2	¬ Tab	(premise)
3	✓ ¬¬$\exists x\ Txb$	(¬ conclusion)
4	$\exists x\ Txb$	(from 3)

None of the rules of inference in Chapter 2 are now applicable. Still, there is an obvious move to make, which is now discussed.

3.1 UNIVERSAL INSTANTIATION ("UI")

Since line 1 says that something is true of all x, that thing must be true in particular of what "b" names. This move is formalized by a new rule of inference, from the universally quantified line 1 of form "$\forall x \ldots x \ldots$" to its instance "$\ldots b \ldots$" in line 5:

1	$\forall x(Txb \to Tab)$	(premise)	$\underline{\forall x \ldots x \ldots}$
5	$(Tbb \to Tab)$	(from 1)	$\ldots b \ldots$

Line 5 was obtained from line 1 by dropping the quantifier "$\forall x$" and replacing "x" by "b."

Note well: Upon applying this new rule ("universal instantiation") we didn't check line 1. That's because checking is a form of erasure; we never return to checked lines. But line 5 doesn't exhaust line 1's implications; line 1 says something about everyone ("If that one can trap Moriarty, Holmes can"), and line 5 says that only about Moriarty ("If Moriarty can trap Moriarty, Holmes can"). If line 1 is true, what it says about everyone must be true not only of Moriarty, but of Holmes, and of any other members of the domain over which the variable "x" ranges, named or anonymous. In general we may wish to draw indefinitely many conclusions "$\ldots a \ldots$," "$\ldots b \ldots$," "$\ldots c \ldots$," and so on from premises of form "$\forall x \ldots x \ldots$." That's why we don't check such premises after any one application of the rule. For the record, here's the rule:

Universal instantiation (UI)	$\underline{\forall x \ldots x \ldots}$
	$\ldots$ any name $\ldots$

If we now apply the rule for conditionals to line 5, the tree splits into two branches, one of which closes immediately:

1	$\forall x\ (Txb \to Tab)$	(premise)
2	$\neg\, Tab$	(premise)
3	$\checkmark\ \neg\neg \exists x\ Txb$	($\neg$ conclusion)
4	$\exists x\ Txb$	(from 3)
5	$\checkmark\ (Tbb \to Tab)$	(from 1)
6	$\neg\, Tbb \qquad Tab$	(from 5)
	$\times$	

At this point the tree is still open, and none of our rules applies usefully; the rule of universal instantiation could be applied with "a" for "x" to derive "$(Tab \rightarrow Tab)$" from line 1, but that's a tautology ("If Holmes can trap Moriarty, then Holmes can trap Moriarty") and can't affect the outcome of the tree test. We need a new rule that can be applied to the assertion in line 4 that someone in the domain of the variable "x" can trap Moriarty.

3.2 EXISTENTIAL INSTANTIATION ("EI")

If all lines in the open path are true, at least one person (x) exists who can trap Moriarty (Txb), as line 4 says. So we choose a name ("c") for that person, and at the bottom of each open path in which line 4 occurs (there's only one) we say about c what line 4 says about x (see line 7 below):

1	$\forall x\,(Txb \rightarrow Tab)$	(premise)	
2	$\neg\,Tab$	(premise)	
3	$\checkmark \neg\neg \exists x\, Txb$	($\neg$ conclusion)	
4	$\checkmark\ \exists x\, Txb$	(from 3)	$\checkmark\ \exists x \ldots x \ldots$
5	$\checkmark\ (Tbb \rightarrow Tab)$	(from 1)	
6	$\neg\,Tbb \qquad Tab$	(from 5)	
7	$Tcb \qquad \times$	(from 4)	$\ldots c \ldots$

Note well: Upon applying this new rule ("existential instantiation"), we did check line 4 and *we used a new name "c"* in line 7 to instantiate the existentially quantified variable "x," *i.e.*, a name that wasn't already used in the path to which we added the instance of line 4. As the name "c" is new to the path, its bearer is an unknown, allowing line 7 ("Tcb") to convey precisely the information that the existentially quantified line 4 conveyed, i.e., *someone or other can trap Moriarty.*

Existential instantiation (EI)	$\exists x \ldots x \ldots$
	$\ldots$ new name $\ldots$

It would have been a mistake to have put "a" or "b" for "x" to get line 7, but because of peculiarities of this example the mistaken step would have given the right result, a closed tree—for the wrong reason, with "Tab" or "Tbb" in line 7 contradicting line 2 or line 6. But in examples like the following the procedural mistake would misclassify an invalid argument as valid:

1	✓ ∃x Tax	Holmes can trap someone
2	¬ Taa	¬ Holmes can trap himself
(3)	Taa	("from 1": WRONG)
	×	

The right move would have used a new letter, say, "b" to get a third (and final) line that leaves the tree open:

    3   Tab

3.3 UI AGAIN—CLOSURE

It's well that we didn't check line 1 when we applied the rule of universal instantiation to it in Section 3.1, for now we have a new name, "c," and, with it, a new instance of line 1, i.e., line 8:

1	∀x (Txb → Tab)	(premise)	∀x…x…
2	¬ Tab	(premise)	
3	✓ ¬¬∃x Txb	(¬ conclusion)	
4	✓ ∃x Txb	(from 3)	
5	✓ (Tbb → Tab)	(from 1)	
6	¬ Tbb Tab	(from 5)	
7	Tcb ×	(from 4)	
8	(Tcb → Tab)	(from 1)	…c…

No matter that earlier we substituted "b" for "x" to get line 5 from line 1; the universally quantified variable "x" in line 1 can stand for anyone at all, including the shadowy c, concerning whom we know only that she or he can trap Moriarty.

If we now apply the rule for conditionals, the tree closes; lines 1 through 3 form an inconsistent set, the inference is valid.

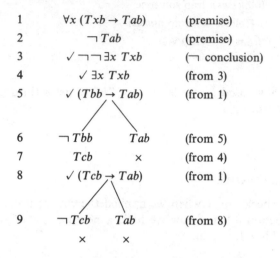

1	$\forall x\,(Txb \to Tab)$	(premise)
2	$\neg Tab$	(premise)
3	$\checkmark \neg\neg\exists x\,Txb$	($\neg$ conclusion)
4	$\checkmark \exists x\,Txb$	(from 3)
5	$\checkmark (Tbb \to Tab)$	(from 1)
6	$\neg Tbb \qquad Tab$	(from 5)
7	$Tcb \qquad \times$	(from 4)
8	$\checkmark (Tcb \to Tab)$	(from 1)
9	$\neg Tcb \qquad Tab$	(from 8)
	$\times \qquad\quad \times$	

3.4 EXAMPLES

Now try the method on the following three arguments. Solutions follow.

(a) If Watson can trap Moriarty, anyone can, $(Tcb \to \forall x Txb)$. Holmes can't, $\neg Tab$. Therefore, Watson can't, $\neg Tcb$.

(b) Everyone is mortal, $\forall x\,Mx$, so no one is immortal, $\neg\exists x\,\neg Mx$.

(c) *Someone* referred the Baron to the Count, $\exists x\,Rxbc$, so it must have been Alma, $Rabc$.

Solutions.

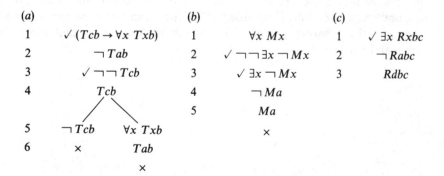

(a)		(b)		(c)	
1	$\checkmark (Tcb \to \forall x\,Txb)$	1	$\forall x\,Mx$	1	$\checkmark \exists x\,Rxbc$
2	$\neg Tab$	2	$\checkmark \neg\neg\exists x\,\neg Mx$	2	$\neg Rabc$
3	$\checkmark \neg\neg Tcb$	3	$\checkmark \exists x\,\neg Mx$	3	$Rdbc$
4	Tcb	4	$\neg Ma$		
		5	Ma		
5	$\neg Tcb \qquad \forall x\,Txb$		$\times$		
6	$\times \qquad\quad Tab$				
	$\times$				

Arguments *a* and *b* are valid, *c* is invalid. Now try to explain why each line is in each of these trees, after the standard opening lines (premises, denied conclusions, results of applying the rule for double denial to conclusions). Then read the following three paragraphs to see whether your explanations are correct.

In (*a*), line 5 comes by applying the rule for conditionals to line 1: $(\bigcirc \rightarrow \triangle)$, with "*Tcb*" for the circle and "$\forall x\ Tbx$" for the triangle. The left branch is closed. Line 6 comes from the right branch of 5 by UI with "*a*" for "*x*." Line 2 denies line 6; the right branch is closed.

In (*b*), line 4 comes from 3 by EI, using the new name "*a*" (any name would be new at this stage), and line 5 comes from 1 by UI with "*a*" for "*x*." Line 4 denies line 5; the tree is closed.

In (*c*), line 3 comes from line 1 by EI, using the new name "*d*." (Use of the old name "*a*" would have closed the tree fallaciously: it needn't have been Alma who reported the Baron to the Count.)

Now try these four; there are solutions at the end of the book.

(*d*) Alma doesn't love the Baron, $\neg\ Lab$, so not everybody does, $\neg\ \forall x\ Lxb$.

(*e*) Everyone loves Alma, so Alma loves herself (*Laa*).

(*f*) Alma, who loves all who love her, doesn't love the Baron, so he doesn't love her:
$\forall x\ (Lxa \rightarrow Lax)$, $\neg\ Lab$, so $\neg\ Lba$.

(*g*) Henry, if anyone, can find Min, $\forall x\ (Mx \rightarrow H)$, so if someone can find Min, Henry can, $(\exists x\ Mx \rightarrow H)$.

Note that in (*g*) the conclusion is of the form $(\bigcirc \rightarrow \triangle)$, with "$\exists x\ Mx$" for the circle and "*H*" for the triangle. *Moral:* The quantifiers "$\forall x$" and "$\exists x$" behave like the sign "$\neg$" of denial in that each of these three is taken to govern as little of the sentence as possible, compatibly with the full sentence making sense. Now let's spell that out formally.

3.5 RULES OF FORMATION

A quantifier is a two-symbol sequence: "$\forall$" or "$\exists$," followed by a variable. In this chapter the only variable we'll use is "x," so the quantifiers we'll be using are just "$\forall x$" and "$\exists x$."

In Section 1.13 we specified capital letters with or without subscripts as the atoms ("starters") from which we constructed larger sentences via denial, conjunction, disjunction, conditioning, and biconditioning. But now we have atomic sentences of other forms, too, e.g., "*Ma*," "*Tab*," "*Rabc*," meaning such things as that the bearer of the name "*a*" can find Min, that Holmes can trap Moriarty, and that Alma referred the Baron to the Count. They have those meanings when the names "*a*," "*b*," "*c*" are suitably interpreted as people and the letters "*M*," "*T*," "*R*" are interpreted as properties (*M*) that people can have or fail to have, or as relations (*T*, *R*) that can hold or fail to hold among people.

Then we need a stock of names, and stocks of sentence letters and symbols for properties of individuals and relations between pairs and triples

of individuals—and beyond, e.g., quadruples as in "*Eabcd*," meaning that
Alma's wealth exceeds the Baron's by twice the amount by which the
Count's falls short of the Duchess's.

In analyzing any particular argument we may need only a finite stock
of such symbols, but there's no telling how large a stock may be needed to
analyze all the arguments we'll meet. Nor is there any point in deciding
once and for all on the shapes of such symbols, or on exactly how they are
to be joined to form sentences. But for now, let's continue to use as names
small letters early in the alphabet, with or without numerical subscripts,
and write them after capital letters, with or without numerical subscripts,
that we'll call "predicates":

"Zero-place predicate" is another way of saying "sentence letter"—0 being
the number of names that need to be appended in order to turn one of those into
something with a truth value, i.e., a sentence.

One-place predicates represent properties of individuals, possible values of the
variable "*x*." Thus, "*M*" above needed to be followed by one name in order to
become a sentence, true or false depending on whether or not the named individual
can find Min.

Two-place predicates stand for relations between pairs of individuals. Thus,
"*Tab*" above was true or false depending on whether or not the one named "*a*" can
trap the one named "*b*."

Three-place predicates stand for relations between triples of such individuals,
as in the sentence "*Rabc*" above.

And so on, for four and more places, without end. When specifying
the logical notation in which an argument is to be analyzed, we always
indicate the number of places that each predicate letter is meant to have,
along with the intended interpretation of the letter and of any names that
are needed—often implicitly, by writing out English sentences ("Holmes
can trap Moriarty," "Watson can't") and translations into logical notation
("*Tab*," "¬ *Tcb*").

We can now revise the rules of formation (see Section 1.13) to cover
quantification as well as truth-functional connectives. This is a matter of
liberalizing rule 0, which in Section 1.13 recognized as atomic sentences
("starters") only zero-place predicates, and adding a new rule (6) for quantifiers. Rules 1 to 5 for connectives are unchanged. As before, the rules specify
(0) an initial stock of sentences, and (1–6) ways of making new ones out of
old ones.

0. *Starters:* Any *n*-place predicate followed by *n* occurrences of names is a sentence. (Examples, with $n - 2$: "*Tab*" and "*Tbb*" but not "*Txb*," because "*x*" is a variable, not a name.)

Six operations on sentences that yield new sentences:

1. *Denial.* Prefix "¬" to any sentence.

2. *Conjunction.* Write "∧" between adjacent members of any sequence of two or more sentences and enclose the result in parentheses.

3. *Disjunction.* Write "∨" between adjacent members of any sequence of two or more sentences and enclose the result in parentheses.

4. *Conditioning.* Write "→" between any two sentences and enclose the result in parentheses.

5. *Biconditioning.* Write "↔" between any two sentences and enclose the result in parentheses.

6. *Quantification.* In a sentence ...*n*... with occurrences of some name *n* but no variables, replace all *n*'s by "*x*"s and then prefix "∀*x*" or "∃*x*." *Example:* That's how "∀*x* (*Txb* → *Tab*)" comes from "(*Tcb* → *Tab*)."

Until further notice (in Chapter 4), nothing counts as a sentence unless its being so follows from rules 0 through 6.

The sentence "∀*x* (*Txb* → *Tab*)" can be parsed by a so-called formation tree as follows, where the parenthesized numbers indicate rules of formation that certify the expressions at the left as sentences.

```
Tcb        Tab       (0)
 |          |
 |          |
(Tcb → Tab)          (4)
      |
∀x (Txb → Tab)       (6)
```

A slight relocation of the opening parentheses changes that to a sentence "(∀*x* *Txb* → *Tab*)" that's parsed very differently:

```
Tcb        Tab       (0)
 |          |
∀x Txb      |        (6)
 |          |
(∀x Txb → Tab)       (4)
```

The first of these sentences is a truth of fact: "Holmes, if anyone, can trap Moriarty." The second is a truth of reason: "If everybody can trap Moriarty, Holmes can." Obscured in idiomatic English, the difference is clear in logical notation.

3.6 THE COMPLETE METHOD, WITH FLOWCHART

Here are the rules of universal and existential instantiation, spelled out in full.

> **Universal instantiation, UI.** Given an open path with a line of form $\forall x \ldots x \ldots$, don't check it, but for any or all names n appearing in the path, write $\ldots n \ldots$ at the bottom unless it already occurs as a line of that path. If no names occur in the path, choose some name n and write $\ldots n \ldots$ at the bottom.

> **Existential instantiation, EI.** Check an unchecked full line of form $\exists x \ldots x \ldots$, and inspect every open path containing it to see if it also contains a line of form $\ldots n \ldots$. If so, let it be; if not, choose a name n that is *new to the path* and write $\ldots n \ldots$ at the bottom.

In these rules $\ldots n \ldots$ is what $\ldots x \ldots$ becomes when all x's in it are replaced by n's.

Warning: These rules are to be applied only to lines that literally begin with quantifiers when written out in full with all parentheses. Thus, UI applies to "$\forall x(Mx \rightarrow H)$" but not to "$\forall x \, Mx \rightarrow H$," which, being an abbreviation of "$(\forall x \, Mx \rightarrow H)$," begins with a parenthesis, not a quantifier. And EI applies to "$\exists x \neg Txb$" but not to "$\neg \exists x \, Txb$."

The rules UI and EI allow us to deal with sentences $\forall x \, \bigcirc$ and $\exists x \, \bigcirc$ as lines of trees. Denials of such sentences are easily handled, simply by rewriting "$\neg \forall x$" as "$\exists x \neg$" and rewriting "$\neg \exists x$" as "$\forall x \neg$." These two new rules, together with the rules for double denial and closure from Chapter 2, are referred to in stage 2 of Figure 3.1.

Rules for $\neg$			$\bigcirc$
$\dfrac{\checkmark \neg \forall x \, \bigcirc}{\exists x \neg \bigcirc}$	$\dfrac{\checkmark \neg \exists x \, \bigcirc}{\forall x \neg \bigcirc}$	$\dfrac{\checkmark \neg \neg \bigcirc}{\bigcirc}$	$\dfrac{\neg \bigcirc}{\times}$

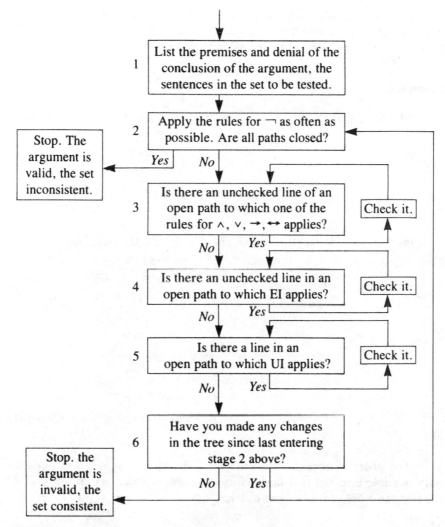

FIGURE 3.1
Flowchart for rules of inference.

It is easy to see why the two new rules are justified: (1) $\neg \forall x\ \bigcirc$ and $\exists x\ \neg \bigcirc$ are logically equivalent because to deny that everything in a non-empty domain has a property is to assert the existence in that domain of something that lacks it; (2) $\neg \exists x\ \bigcirc$ and $\forall x\ \neg \bigcirc$ are logically equivalent because to deny the existence in a domain of things having a property is to assert that everything there lacks it.

It follows that "$\neg \exists x\ \neg$" has the same meaning as "$\forall x$," and that "$\neg \forall x\ \neg$" has the same meaning as "$\exists x$."

Our rules of inference are now complete, relative to the logical notation now at hand; they allow us to test the validity of any argument, and the consistency of any set of sentences, in that notation.

Examples.

(a) $\forall x\ Mx$, so $\exists x\ Mx$.

1	$\forall x\ Mx$	
2	$\checkmark \neg \exists x\ Mx$	
3	$\checkmark \forall x \neg Mx$	(from 2)
4	$\neg Ma$	(from 3)
5	Ma	(from 1)
	$\times$	

(b) $\exists x\ Mx \to H$, so $\forall x\ (Mx \to H)$.

1	$\checkmark \exists x\ Mx \to H$	
2	$\checkmark \neg \forall x\ (Mx \to H)$	
3	$\checkmark \exists x \neg (Mx \to H)$	(from 2)
4	$\checkmark \neg (Ma \to H)$	(from 3)
5	Ma	(from 4)
6	$\neg H$	(from 4)
7	$\checkmark \neg \exists x\ Mx \qquad H$	(from 1)
8	$\forall x \neg Mx \qquad \times$	(from 7)
9	$\neg Ma$	(from 8)
	$\times$	

The order of application of the rules shown in Figure 3.1 is not the only possible one, but it is fairly efficient (usually) and does ensure that if the tree can close, it will, sooner or later.

3.7 LOGICAL STRUCTURE

Let us now reexamine the argument studied at length at the beginning of this chapter:

Holmes, if anyone, can trap Moriarty. Holmes can't. Therefore, no one can.

We symbolized this as follows.

$$\forall x\ (Txb \to Tab),\ \neg Tab,\ so\ \neg \exists x\ Txb.$$

But that symbolization displays more of the logical structure of premises and conclusion than is needed to establish validity. Thus, instead of the two-place predicate "T" for "can trap" in "Tab" (Holmes can trap Moriarty) and "Txb" (x can trap Moriarty), we could have used a one-place predicate "M," with "Ma" meaning that Holmes can trap Moriarty and "Mx" meaning that x can. The tree test shows this version of the argument to be valid:

$\forall x \, (Mx \rightarrow Ma)$ (premise)

$\quad \neg Ma$ (premise)

$\checkmark \; \neg \neg \exists x \, Mx$ ($\neg$ conclusion)

$\quad \checkmark \exists x \, Mx$

$\qquad Mb$

$\quad Mb \rightarrow Ma$

$\neg Mb \qquad Ma$

$\quad \times \qquad\quad \times$

And even this symbolization shows more structure than is needed to see that the argument is valid. If we write "Holmes can trap Moriarty" simply as "H," the argument still passes the tree test:

$\forall x \, (Mx \rightarrow H)$ (premise)

$\quad \neg H$ (premise)

$\checkmark \; \neg \neg \exists x \, Mx$ ($\neg$ conclusion)

$\quad \checkmark \exists x \, Mx$

$\qquad Ma$

$\quad Ma \rightarrow H$

$\neg Ma \qquad H$

$\quad \times \qquad\quad \times$

This form "$\forall x \, (Mx \rightarrow H)$, $\neg H$, so $\neg \exists x \, Mx$" shows only as much of the logical structure of premises and conclusion as is needed to demonstrate validity of the argument—given that the first premise, "Holmes, if anyone, can trap Moriarty," is construed as a universally quantified sentence, $\forall x \ldots x \ldots$.

But we could have begun on a very different track, construing that premise as a conditional with existentially quantified antecedent, say,

"$(\exists x\ Mx \rightarrow H)$," which we saw in Sections 3.6, example b, and 3.4, example g, to imply and be implied by "$\forall x\ (Mx \rightarrow H)$":

(Someone can trap Moriarty $\rightarrow$ Holmes can trap Moriarty)

$\neg$ Holmes can trap Moriarty.

$\neg$ Someone can trap Moriarty

Now here the structure of that antecedent plays no role in closing the tree; writing the argument as "$S \rightarrow H, \neg H$, so $\neg S$," the tree test of Chapter 2 would have found it valid:

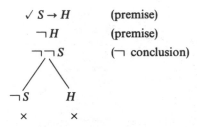

$\sqrt{}\ S \rightarrow H$ (premise)

$\neg H$ (premise)

$\neg\neg S$ ($\neg$ conclusion)

$\neg S$ H

$\times$ $\times$

Then by judiciously rephrasing before symbolizing it, we might have shown this argument to be valid without using the new notation and rules of this chapter; but more commonly, arguments that seem to involve quantifiers really do involve them, and no amount of rephrasing will turn them into arguments that can be symbolized adequately and tested by the methods of Chapter 2.

3.8 PROBLEMS

1. Test validity by the tree method.
   (*a*) Alma paints, so someone does: Pa, so $\exists x\ Px$.
   (*b*) Someone paints, so Alma does.
   (*c*) Alma loves someone, for she loves the Baron.
   (*d*) Of course Alma loves herself—everyone does: $\forall x\ Lxx$, so Laa.
   (*e*) Someone sings, so someone paints, for all singers paint:
        $\exists x\ Sx, \forall x\ (Sx \rightarrow Px)$, so $\exists x\ Px$.

2. Test validity by the tree method.
   (*a*) Since everyone loves Alma, Alma loves someone: $\forall x\ Lxa$, so $\exists x\ Lax$.
   (*b*) Since Alma loves the Baron, and he loves everyone who loves her, he loves himself: $Lab, \forall x\ (Lxa \rightarrow Lbx)$, so Lbb.
   (*c*) Alma loves some who love her, for she loves herself: Laa, so $\exists x\ (Lxa \land Lax)$.
   (*d*) Not everyone loves Alma, for she loves everyone who loves her, but does not love everyone: $\forall x\ (Lxa \rightarrow Lax), \neg\forall x\ Lax$, so $\neg\forall x\ Lxa$.

3. By the tree method, test each pair for logical equivalence.
   (*a*) Alma does not love all her lovers: $\neg\forall x\ (Lxa \rightarrow Lax)$.

Alma has a lover whom she does not love: $\exists x \, (Lxa \land \neg \, Lax)$.

(b) All who are loved by Alma love her: $\forall x \, (Lax \to Lxa)$.

If Alma loves all, all love her: $(\forall x \, Lax \to \forall x \, Lxa)$.

4. Draw formation trees for the four sentences in problem 3.

5. "Since Alma's no fool, and no fool plays chess, Alma plays chess": $\neg \, Fa$, $\forall x \, (Fx \to \neg \, Cx)$, so Ca. Is that valid? Do a tree.

6. *Who am I?* (Find a snappy conclusion that closes the tree.)

(a) "Everybody loves baby, but baby loves nobody but me":
$\forall x \, Lxb$, $\forall x \, (Lbx \to Ixa)$. ("$Ixa$," x is me.)

(b) "Brothers and sisters have I none, but that man's father is my father's son":
$\forall x \, (Bbx \to Ixa)$, Bbc. ("B," begat; "a," me; "b," my father; "c," that man's father.)

7. Symbolize the following argument, and test validity by the tree method. Is it sound? What are the truth values of its premises? "This argument is unsound, for its conclusion is false, and no sound argument has a false conclusion."

3.9 INTERPRETATIONS

"A valid argument is one whose conclusion is true in every case in which all its premises are true." That's how we began. In the truth-functional logic of Chapters 1 and 2 these cases were assignments of truth values to sentence letters. On that basis we were able to devise and prove adequate an efficient tree method for testing validity of arguments and consistency of sets of sentences. We have now extended that method to deal with generalized sentences in which quantifiers "$\forall x$" and "$\exists x$" apply to inscriptions like "Lax" and "$(Lax \to Lxa)$" that would be sentences if the variable "x" were replaced by a name. To understand that extension we need to extend the notion of case so as to make sense when atomic sentences need not be sentence letters (zero-place predicates, so to speak) but may also be formed by writing names singly or in twos or threes, etc., after *n*-place predicates where *n* is 1 or 2 or 3, etc.

What can we assign to predicate letters with one or more places, to do the work done by assigning truth values to sentence letters—the work of defining "case" in a way that makes sense of the definition of validity as absence of counterexamples? Answer: *extensions*, i.e., the sets of things they are true of. To specify a case we shall have to give such an answer for each predicate letter that appears in the argument. We shall also have to specify the domain over which the variable "x" ranges. And for each name that appears in the argument we shall have to specify an extension (a bearer) in that domain.

The domain will be some set of items—people, vertebrates, numbers, places, times—whatever. When we need a general name for such items, of unknown or unnamed kinds, we'll call them "individuals." Our only requirement is that there be at least one individual, so that the domain is not empty. When arguments are given in English, the general character of the domain is indicated by linguistic features such as pronouns: "Min is home, so *someone* is" makes it clear that Min is not the family cat but a person, so that when the argument is symbolized "*Ha*, so ∃x *Hx*," we understand that the domain is to be some set of people, one of whom, Min, is the "*a*" of the premise. Some of the small letters "*a*," "*b*," etc., will name individuals in the domain, as when "*a*" names Min here. In specifying a case, we designate particular individuals as extensions of whatever letters are used as names.

Example 1. In a discussion of the Roman emperors before the division of the empire we might read "*a*" as Augustus and "*T*" as the property of being one of the first three emperors. We specify this interpretation as follows.

Domain:	{Augustus, Tiberius, Caligula, ..., Theodosius}
Extension of "*a*":	Augustus
Extension of "*T*":	{Augustus, Tiberius, Caligula}

(Members of sets are indicated in braces, curly brackets.) That's how we specify a case when predicate letters have just one place.

Example 2. Two-place predicate letters like "*L*" in discussions of Alma's aristocratic love life are true of pairs, in each of which the first member loves the second in the case in question. Thus, since Alma loves the Baron in the case we shall now define, the predicate "*L*" is true of the pair indicated by "(Alma, Baron)."

Domain:	{Alma, the Baron, the Count, the Duchess, the Earl}
Extension of "*a*":	Alma
Extension of "*b*":	the Baron
Extension of "*c*":	the Count.
Extension of "*L*":	{(Alma, the Baron), (the Baron, the Count), (the Count, Alma)}

In this case the five individuals include only three lovers, who form an unhappy circle: Alma loves only the Baron, who loves only the Count, who loves only Alma. The Duchess and the Earl neither love nor are loved. (Nor are they assigned names, in this case.)

Example 3. With "*R*" a three-place predicate where, say, "*Rabc*" means that Alma referred the Baron to the Count, we might specify a case as follows—a case in which Alma refers the Baron and the Count to each other, and nobody refers anybody else to anybody.

Domain: {Alma, the Baron, the Count, the Duchess, the Earl}

Extension of "*R*": {(Alma, the Baron, the Count), (Alma, the Count, the Baron)}

Since none of the individuals in the domain are assigned names in this case, we can't describe the case precisely, in logical notation; but the sentence "$\neg \exists x\ Rxxx$" does describe a certain general feature of the case. Other general features can be described only by using more variables, as in Chapter 4: "$\exists x\ \exists y\ \exists z\ (Rxyz \wedge Rxzy)$."

3.10 RULES OF INTERPRETATION

Now we can parallel the rules of formation of Section 3.5 with rules for determining the truth values of sentences in a case *C*, given its domain and what the names refer to and what the predicate letters are true of in *C*.

---

0. *Starters.* An atomic sentence $\bigcirc$ (an *n*-place predicate letter followed by *n* names) is true or false in a case *C* depending on whether or not the *n*-tuple of extensions that *C* assigns to the successive names belongs to the extension that *C* assigns to the predicate letter. (If $n = 0$, *C* simply assigns t or f to $\bigcirc$.)

If $\bigcirc$ and $\triangle$ are sentences, the truth values of their compounds in *C* are determined as follows:

1. *Denial,* $\neg \bigcirc$: truth value opposite to that of $\bigcirc$.

2. *Conjunction,* $(\bigcirc \wedge \triangle)$: t iff $\bigcirc$ and $\triangle$ are both t.

3. *Disjunction,* $(\bigcirc \vee \triangle)$: f iff $\bigcirc$ and $\triangle$ are both f.

4. *Conditional,* $(\bigcirc \to \triangle)$: f iff $\bigcirc$ is t and $\triangle$ is f.

5. *Biconditional,* $(\bigcirc \leftrightarrow \triangle)$: t iff $\bigcirc$ and $\triangle$ agree in truth value.

In rules 6a and 6b the sentence $\bigcirc$ is of form $\forall x \ldots x \ldots$ or $\exists x \ldots x \ldots$, *name* is some name to which *C* assigns no extension, and C_i is just like *C* except for assigning *i* as extension to that name.

6a. *Universal quantification.* *C* assigns t to $\forall x \ldots x \ldots$ iff for every individual *i* in the common domain of cases *C* and C_i, case C_i assigns t to $\ldots$ *name* $\ldots$.

6b. *Existential quantification.* *C* assigns t to $\exists x \ldots x \ldots$ iff for some individual *i* in the common domain of cases *C* and C_i, case C_i assigns t to $\ldots$ *name* $\ldots$.

3.11   COUNTEREXAMPLES

Now let us see how open paths in finished trees involving general statements determine cases in which all sentences in such paths are true, so that
in tests of validity the premises and denied conclusions at the beginnings of
such paths are true in those cases.

As an example, consider the invalid argument "$\exists x\ Fxa$, so Fba" from
the premise "Someone fears Alma" to the conclusion that the Baron does.
Here's the tree:

1	$\checkmark\ \exists x\ Fxa$	(premise)
2	$\neg\ Fba$	($\neg$ conclusion)
3	Fca	(from 1—by EI, requiring a new name)

The tree is finished; in the flow chart of Figure 3.1 we end in the " Stop"
box at the lower left, indicating that there are cases in which all lines of the
path are true. One such case, C, is defined as follows.

Extensions of names: The extension of the ith name to appear in the path is
the number i. Then "a" names 1, "b" names 2, "c" names 3.

Domain: The set $\{1, 2, 3\}$ of the numbers so named.

Extension of "F": This contains the pair (i, j) if and only if some full line of
the path is an atomic sentence consisting of "F" followed by names whose extensions are i and j in that order. There's only one such atomic sentence, line 3, so "F"
is true of the pair $(3, 1)$ only. Then the extension of "F" is the set $\{(3, 1)\}$.

Now in case C, all three lines of the path are true. That's so because
according to rule 0 of interpretation, lines 2 and 3 are true, and because
truth of line 1—"*Someone* fears Alma," or "'F' is true of *some* pair $(i, 1)$"—
follows from truth of line 3, "The Count fears Alma," or "'F' is true of the
pair $(3, 1)$."

This last argument, from truth of line 3 to truth of line 1, may seem
backward. Shouldn't it be the other way around? Didn't line 3 come from
line 1, by the rule of inference EI? Sure it did, but EI is a funny rule,
unsound (in the sense of Section 2.7) but complete. Unsound: the argument
from its premise "$\exists x\ Fxa$" to its conclusion "Fca" is invalid. It's the argument in the other direction, from "Fca" to "$\exists x\ Fxa$," that's valid, truth-
preserving. That's completeness of the rule, which is exactly what we need
for present purposes, drawing truth in C up the tree from lower lines to the
higher lines we got them from as conclusions. The argument that draws up
truth in C of line 1 from truth in C of line 3 goes backward, from conclusion "...*name*..." to premise "$\exists x\ ...x...$" of the rule EI.

Another example.

$$\exists x\ Px$$

$$\exists x\ Qx$$

$$\exists x\ (Px \wedge Qx)$$

—as it might be, "Someone's up, someone's down, so someone's up and down." There are three full paths through the finished tree.

1	✓ $\exists x\ Px$	(premise)
2	✓ $\exists x\ Qx$	(premise)
3	✓ $\neg \exists x\ (Px \wedge Qx)$	($\neg$ conclusion)
4	Pa	(from 1)
5	Qb	(from 2)
6	$\forall x\ \neg(Px \wedge Qx)$	(from 3)
7	✓ $\neg(Pa \wedge Qa)$	(from 6)
8	✓ $\neg(Pb \wedge Qb)$	(from 6)
9	$\neg Pa$ $\neg Qa$	(from 7)
10	$\neg Pb$ $\neg Qb$	(from 8)

Only the middle path is open. It determines this interpretation, C:

Domain:	$\{1, 2\}$
Extensions of "a," "b":	1, 2
Extension of "P":	$\{1\}$
Extension of "Q":	$\{2\}$

So to speak, interpretation C injects truth or falsehood into atomic sentences depending on whether or not they are full lines of the path. EI's completeness then draws truth in C up from atomic sentences 4 and 5 to lines 1 and 2, whence they came by EI. Completeness of the rule for denied quantifiers draws truth in C up to line 3 from line 6, which draws truth up from the lines (7 and 8) that come from it by UI—not because UI is complete (it isn't), but because in C the items named by "a" and "b" exhaust the domain, so that what's true of both of them is true of everything. Finally, completeness of the rule for denied disjunctions draws truth in C

up to lines 7 and 8 from denials of atomic sentences, i.e., lines 9 and 10. The flow of truth is shown in Figure 3.2.

Then in case C, all lines in the open path are true—including lines 1 to 3, the premises and denied conclusion of the argument, so that C is a counterexample.

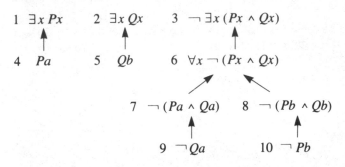

FIGURE 3.2
Drawing up truth.

What makes this go is the fact that our rules of inference are complete or—in the case of UI—close enough to being complete:

> **Path completeness.** Suppose that in an open path through a finished tree all lines that come from a certain line as conclusions of one of the tree rules are true *in the particular interpretation C that the path determines*, in which the true atomic sentences (if any) are the ones that appear as full lines of the path. Then the premise, the line from which they come, is also true in C.

The reason, illustrated above, is that if in a finished tree $\forall x \ldots x \ldots$ is a line of an open path, so is every sentence $\ldots n \ldots$ for which n is a name in the path. Since every individual in C's domain is named in the path, $\forall x \ldots x \ldots$ is then true in C if all the sentences $\ldots n \ldots$ are.

3.12 "SOME S's ARE P"

It's a common error to imagine that since the difference between English sentences of forms "All S's are P" and "Some S's are P" is just the difference between the adjectives "all" and "some," the corresponding sentences in logical notation differ only in the quantifiers "$\forall x$" and "$\exists x$," and that since "All S's are P" goes over into logical notation as "$\forall x (Sx \rightarrow Px)$," "Some S's are P" must go over as "$\exists x (Sx \rightarrow Px)$." But in fact "Some S's are P" means that at least one individual is both S and P: $\exists x (Sx \land Px)$.

Problem. Show that although the argument from "∃x (Sx ∧ Px)" to "∃x (Sx → Px)" is valid, the argument in the other direction isn't:

There's something that's practical if it's a sloop.   ∃x (Sx → Px)

There's a practical sloop.   ∃x (Sx ∧ Px)

You'll find that there are three open paths through the finished tree. Describe the counterexamples that those paths determine, and satisfy yourself that in each of them it's the false conclusion "∃x (Sx ∧ Px)" rather than the true premise "∃x (Sx → Px)" that has the same truth value as "Some S's are P." (For a solution, see Section 3.16.)

3.13 DECIDABILITY

The adequacy proofs at the end of Chapter 2 are easily adapted to sentences and arguments involving the quantifiers "∀x" and "∃x." The ingredients are soundness, completeness, and decidability. Reversing the order, we start with decidability:

> If the initial list is finite, the tree test always terminates after some finite number of steps.

When UI is applied to lines ∀x ...x..., quantifiers never appear in the resulting lines ...*name*.... That'll change in Chapter 4, but in this chapter tree tests will always terminate after a finite number of steps, because the number of progeny that a line ∀x ...x... can have is limited by the number of names and existential quantifiers in the initial list. Here, then, after a finite number of applications of UI and EI we shall be dealing with a tree to which only the rules of Chapter 2 apply, so that by the census argument of Section 2.8 we must eventually reach a decision in one of the flow graph's "Stop" boxes.

3.14 COMPLETENESS

> If there's an open path through the finished tree, the initial list is consistent.

That's true because of the path completeness defined at the end of Section 3.11.

Recall that in C the successive names in the open path denote successive positive integers, the domain of the variables is the set of all integers so denoted, and the extension of each *n*-place predicate letter is only what it must be in order to make truths in *C* of all atomic sentences with that predicate letter that appear as full lines of the path. Thus all lines of the path that are atomic sentences are true in *C*, as are all lines that are denials of atomic sentences, since the atomic sentences following those denial signs must be false in *C*. And path completeness transmits the property of truth in *C* up the tree from conclusions to premises of rules of inference. Eventually that process will reach the initial lines of the tree, which are thereby shown to be consistent, true in some case, viz., *C*.

3.15 SOUNDNESS

> If the initial list is consistent, there's an open path through the finished tree.

That's because the property of having all lines true in a particular interpretation is transmitted from an open path to at least one of its prolongations when a rule of inference is applied to a line of the path. Any path in which all lines are true in some interpretation is open, i.e., doesn't contain both a sentence $\bigcirc$ and its denial $\neg\,\bigcirc$ as full lines, for one or the other would have have to be false in the interpretation.

As the initial list is consistent, there is an interpretation in which all its lines are true—an interpretation *C* that assigns extensions to all names that appear in the list, and to no names that don't.* By soundness of the rules of inference other than EI, we know that when one of them is applied to a line of the path, all lines in at least one of the path's prolongations are also true in that interpretation. If the path is extended by applying EI to a line $\exists x \ldots x \ldots$, the new line $\ldots name \ldots$ will contain a name to which *C* assigns no extension. Now let C_i be an interpretation just like *C* except for assigning as extension to *name* an individual *i* so as to make the new line true in C_i. Since the line $\exists x \ldots x \ldots$ was true in *C*, there is such an individual.

Thus the property of having all lines true in some interpretation trickles down from open paths to prolongations when rules of inference are applied.

---

* If the interpretation makes all lines true but assigns extensions to names that appear in none of them, just drop the extensions of the extra names, leaving everything else alone—domain, extensions of predicate letters. This trimmed interpretation will still make all lines true.

3.16 "SOME *S*'s ARE *P*": SOLUTION

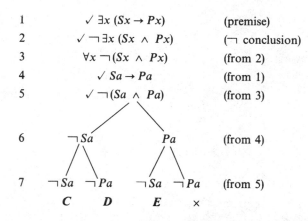

1	$\checkmark\ \exists x\ (Sx \to Px)$	(premise)
2	$\checkmark\ \neg\exists x\ (Sx \wedge Px)$	($\neg$ conclusion)
3	$\forall x\ \neg(Sx \wedge Px)$	(from 2)
4	$\checkmark\ Sa \to Pa$	(from 1)
5	$\checkmark\ \neg(Sa \wedge Pa)$	(from 3)

6   $\neg Sa$ Pa (from 4)

7   $\neg Sa$ $\neg Pa$ $\neg Sa$ $\neg Pa$ (from 5)
     C   *D*   *E*   ×

Call the interpretations determined by the open paths "*C*," "*D*," and "*E*," as indicated. In each, the domain is the set $\{1\}$, and the extension of "*a*" is 1. In *C* and *D*, neither "*S*" nor "*P*" is true of anything, since no full line of either path is an atomic sentence. Then the paths determine the same interpretation; $C = D$. In *E*, "*P*" is true of 1, since "*Pa*" in a full line of that path, and since "*Sa*" isn't, "*S*" is true of nothing. Evidently it's the falsity of "*Sa*" in all three interpretations that makes the premise "$\exists x\ (Sx \to Px)$" true and the conclusion "$\exists x\ (Sx \wedge Px)$" false, for as "*a*" names the sole element of the domain, these agree in truth value with "$Sa \to Pa$" and "$Sa \wedge Pa$," respectively. With "*Sa*" false, the first of these is true and the second false. In terms of sloops and practicality, the interpretations say that there are no sloops, so it's surely false that some sloops are practical (or impractical, or anything else); it's "$\exists x\ (Sx \wedge Px)$," not "$\exists x\ (Sx \to Px)$," that's got the same truth value as "Some sloops are practical."

For the record, here are the interpretations in official format.

C, D:	Domain:	$\{1\}$
	Extension of "*a*":	1
	Extension of "*S*":	$\emptyset$ (the empty set)
	Extension of "*P*":	$\emptyset$
E:	Domain:	$\{1\}$
	Extension of "*a*":	1
	Extension of "*S*":	$\emptyset$
	Extension of "*P*":	$\{1\}$ (the whole domain)

$$4$$

MULTIPLE GENERALITY

We shall have occasion to use letters other than "x" as variables, and for each of these, say, "y," we have a rule for "$\forall y$" and a rule for "$\exists y$." These will simply be the rules given in Section 3.6 for $\forall x$ and $\exists x$, but with "y" in place of "x" throughout. The domain of the variables may differ from case to case, but in any one case all variables have a common domain. Then the same name (e.g., "a") can be used in all versions of UI:

$$\frac{\forall x \ldots x \ldots}{\ldots a \ldots} \qquad \frac{\forall y \ldots y \ldots}{\ldots a \ldots} \qquad \frac{\forall z \ldots z \ldots}{\ldots a \ldots}$$

4.1 EXAMPLE

Consider the argument "Everybody is related to everybody, so everybody is related to herself or himself." If we take the domain over which the variables "x" and "y" range to be the set of all people, and if we interpret "Rxy" as meaning that x is related to y, the argument goes over into genderless logical notation as

$$\frac{\forall x \, \forall y \, Rxy}{\forall x \, Rxx}$$

The premise is to be interpreted as if it had been written "$\forall x \, (\forall y \, Rxy)$," just as "$\neg \neg H$" is interpreted as if it had been written "$\neg (\neg H)$," but in neither case are the signs of grouping needed, for no other interpretation makes sense. The tree test shows this argument to be valid:

1	$\forall x \, \forall y \, Rxy$	(premise)	$\forall x \ldots x \ldots$
2	$\checkmark \ \neg \forall x \, Rxx$	($\neg$ conclusion)	
3	$\checkmark \ \exists x \, \neg Rxx$	(from 2)	
4	$\neg Raa$	(from 3)	
5	$\forall y \, Ray$	(from 1)	$\ldots a \ldots \qquad \forall y \ldots y \ldots$
6	Raa	(from 5)	$\ldots a \ldots$
	$\times$		

Line 5 came from line 1 by UI, stripping the initial quantifier off "$\forall x \, \forall y \, Rxy$" and replacing the remaining "x" by "a." Line 6 then came from line 5 by UI, stripping the initial quantifier off "$\forall y \, Ray$" and replacing the remaining "y" by the same name, "a." There is no requirement that different variables stand for different items; the only requirement is that different occurrences of the same variable in a sentence stand for the same item.

4.2 EXAMPLE

$$\exists x \, \forall y \, Lxy$$
$$\forall y \, \exists x \, Lxy$$

If the common domain of the two variables is the set of all people, and if "Lxy" means that x loves y, this argument goes over into English as:

There is someone who loves everyone.

Everyone is loved (by someone or other).

That's valid: if someone (named "a," say) loves everyone, then indeed everyone is loved—by a, anyway, and perhaps by others as well. Here's the tree test:

1	$\checkmark \ \exists x \, \forall y \, Lxy$	(premise)
2	$\checkmark \ \neg \forall y \, \exists x \, Lxy$	($\neg$ conclusion)
3	$\checkmark \ \exists y \, \neg \exists x \, Lxy$	(from 2)
4	$\checkmark \ \forall y \, Lay$	(from 1)

5	$\checkmark \neg \exists x \ Lxb$	(from 3)
6	$\forall x \ \neg \ Lxb$	(from 5)
7	$\neg \ Lab$	(from 6)
8	Lab	(from 4)
	×	

It is essential that the rules UI and EI be applied only when the quantifier begins the line. Thus, UI cannot be applied to line 1 above, nor can UI or EI be applied to line 2.

4.3 LOGIC INTO ENGLISH

The information conveyed in logical notation by the order of quantifiers is conveyed in English by a variety of devices. The most reliable way to translate logical notation into English is to begin with the ponderous readings:

for every x there is an x such that

of the quantifiers "$\forall x$" and "$\exists x$" and then work toward idiomatic English in stages. Thus, reading "Lxy" as "x loves y," the sentence "$\forall x \ \exists y \ Lxy$" might first be rendered in near English as:

For every x there is a y such that x loves y
  $\forall x$ $\exists y$ Lxy

To turn this into English we must eliminate the variables and find another way of doing their job of cross-indexing. A clumsy but reliable expedient is to replace the variable in each of the quantifying phrases by a common noun for individuals in the domain—"one," perhaps, in the present example—and writing "the former" and "the latter" for later occurrences of "x" and "y":

For everyone   there is someone such that   the former loves the latter
  $\forall x$ $\exists y$ Lxy

This is English of a sort. It remains only to improve the style, by methods that belong not to logic but to the art of English composition. The clearest expressions of this statement in English seem to be:

Everyone loves.   Everyone is a lover.

These achieve clarity by burying the existential quantifier. The version "Everyone loves someone" shows both quantifiers on the surface, but might (?) be misinterpreted as meaning that everyone loves the same person: all love one.

4.4 LINKAGE

Each of the sentences:

$$\forall x\, \exists y\, Lxy \qquad \forall y\, \exists x\, Lyx$$

goes over into the same clumsy English sentence, "For everyone there is someone such that the former loves the latter." The only purpose of the variables in the first two sentences is to show which member of the pair, lover or beloved, is governed by each quantifier. In clumsy English this job of cross-indexing is done by the locutions "the former" and "the latter." In logical notation it is done in a way that can be clarified by actually drawing links between quantifiers and the variables they govern. The two sentences above are logically equivalent because they show the same pattern of links:

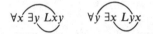

All cross-indexing is shown by the links alone:

$$\forall \; \exists \; L$$

Indeed, we could express the claim that everybody is a lover without using variables at all by adopting the link notation just shown. But for typographical reasons it is convenient to identify the links without actually showing them. We do this by writing the same variable at the two ends of each link, taking care to do this in a way that makes it possible to reconstruct the original pattern of links. This is illustrated in Figure 4.1, where we use the letter "z" for the upper link and "x" for the lower. Writing these letters in place of the ends, we have an expression from which the links can be recovered. The order in which quantifiers are written at the beginning of a sentence can be significant, as can the position after "L" governed by each quantifier. But all relevant information about order and position can be shown without variables, as in the link notation. The decision about what variable to use in the standard notation is a completely trivial one; all that matters is that the intended linkage pattern be determined unambiguously.

Of course, a single quantifier may govern two or more positions

$$\forall z\, \exists x\, Lzx$$

FIGURE 4.1
From unlabeled links to unlinked labels.

within a sentence. "Alma loves everyone who loves her" may be translated as "$\forall x\,(Lxa \to Lax)$," where the quantifier governs the first position after the first "L" and the second after the second:

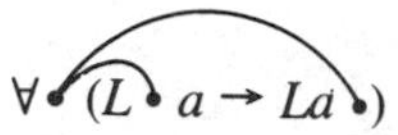

$$\forall \overset{\frown}{(L\,{}^\bullet\,a \to La\,{}^\bullet)}$$

Generalizing "Alma" as in "Someone loves everyone who loves her" yields the more complex example of Figure 4.2.

$$\exists y \forall x\,(Lxy \to Lyx) \qquad \exists\,\,\forall\,\overset{\frown}{(L\,{}^\bullet{}_\bullet \to L\,{}_\bullet{}^\bullet)}$$

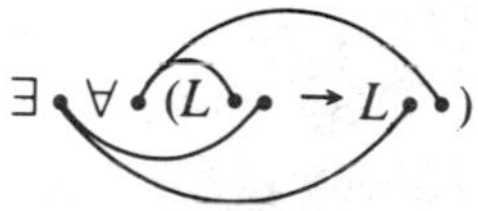

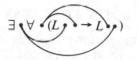

FIGURE 4.2
"Some love all who love them."

The very different statement that someone is loved by everyone she loves has the same order of quantifiers but a different linkage pattern, as shown in Figure 4.3.

$$\exists y \forall x\,(Lyx \to Lxy) \qquad \exists\,\,\forall\,\overset{\frown}{(L\,{}_\bullet{}^\bullet \to L\,{}^\bullet{}_\bullet)}$$

FIGURE 4.3
"There's someone whose love is always reciprocated."

4.5   RULES OF FORMATION

Now that we use variables other than "x," we'll need to update the quantifier rule, rule 6 in Section 3.5, as follows. The rest need not be changed.

---

0. *Starters:* Any n-place predicate followed by n names (counting repetitions) is a sentence. Example: "*Laa*."

Six operations on sentences that yield new sentences:

1. *Denial.* Prefix "$\neg$."
2. *Conjunction.* Infix "$\wedge$," enclose in parentheses.
3. *Disjunction.* Infix "$\vee$," enclose in parentheses.
4. *Conditioning.* Infix "$\to$," enclose in parentheses.
5. *Biconditioning.* Infix "$\leftrightarrow$," enclose in parentheses.
6. *Quantification.* Throughout a sentence, replace a particular name by a variable v that doesn't appear in the sentence, and prefix a universally or existentially quantified v. That quantifier governs (is linked to) all the v's in the resulting sentence, and it continues to govern those same v's in sentences obtained from that resulting sentence by any of these six operations.

Until further notice (in Chapter 5), nothing counts as a sentence unless its being so follows from rules 0 to 6.

The formation tree for "$\forall x\, (\exists y\, Lxy \to \forall y\, Lyx)$" in Figure 4.4 illustrates how the clauses about linkage (government) work, in rule 6. (Choice of "Lca" as a starter was somewhat arbitrary; "Lba" would do as well.)

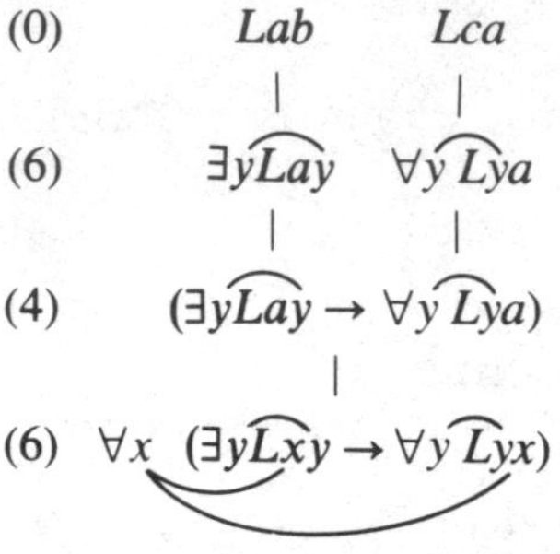

(0) Lab Lca

            | |

(6) $\exists y \overparen{Lay}$ $\forall y\, \overparen{Lya}$

            | |

(4) $(\exists y \overparen{Lay} \to \forall y\, \overparen{Lya})$

            |

(6) $\forall x\, (\exists y \overparen{Lxy} \to \forall y\, \overparen{Lyx})$

FIGURE 4.4
"All the world loves a lover." Formation tree and linkage pattern.

4.6   ENGLISH INTO LOGICAL NOTATION

"All the world loves a lover" (i.e., everybody loves every lover). That's an unexpectedly strong statement; it implies that if there is even one lover, then all love all. We construct a tree for that argument in Section 4.8. Meanwhile, let's see how to go about symbolizing such things.

In a mixture of logical notation and English, the premise is

$$\forall x\, (x \text{ is a lover} \to \text{everyone loves } x)$$

To be a lover is to love someone. Then the antecedent of the conditional is "$\exists y\, x$ loves y" or, in full logical notation, "$\exists y\, Lxy$." And the consequent of the conditional is "$\forall y\, y$ loves x" or "$\forall z\, z$ loves x"—any variable but "x" will do—so that in full logical notation it's, say, "$\forall y\, Lyx$." Then we've done it: the whole premise is

$$\forall x\, (\forall y\, Lxy \to \forall y\, Lyx)$$

That looks fairly nasty if you come upon it all at once, but if you build up to it a step at a time, it makes sense. If you do come upon it all at once, you can decipher it by working backward along the lines suggested in Section 4.3.

The amazing consequence "If there's even one lover then all love all" is simpler; it's a conditional $\bigcirc \to \triangle$ that you can translate simply by translating $\bigcirc$ and $\triangle$. Now $\bigcirc$ is "$\exists x\, x$ is a lover," which we know to be "$\exists x\, \exists y\, Lxy$," and $\triangle$ is "For all x and y, x loves y," i.e., "$\forall x\, \forall y\, Lxy$." Then the whole is

$$\exists x\, \exists y\, Lxy \to \forall x\, \forall y\, Lxy$$

If someone is a lover, then all love all.

Here is a logically equivalent variant:

$$\forall z \, (\exists y \, Lzy \to \forall x \, \forall y \, Lxy)$$

If anyone is a lover, then all love all.

(Compare this with "Holmes, if anyone, can trap Moriarty" as a version of "If someone can trap Moriarty, Holmes can.) That's one of the devices English deploys to do the work of parentheses: "anyone" is used in place of "everyone" to indicate that the whole conditional is to be governed, not just the antecedent. "If *everyone* is a lover, then all love all" goes into logical notation as a very different statement "$(\forall x \, \exists y \, Lxy \to \forall x \, \forall y \, Lxy)$," which doesn't have the astounding consequence that would follow if the left parenthesis were moved right to come just before "$\exists y$."*

Now let's try some truth trees.

4.7   EXAMPLE: ALMA'S NARCISSISM INFLAMES THE BARON

All love all lovers.
Alma loves herself.
_____

The Baron loves Alma.

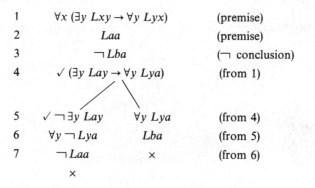

Line 4 comes from line 1 by UI. That's a matter of dropping the universal quantifier "$\forall x$" and changing all remaining "x"s to "a"s.

Even though it was used there as an instance of the variable "x," the name "a" can thereafter be used as an instance of a different variable, e.g.,

_____

* The rules of formation don't actually allow us to form "$\forall x \, (\exists y \, Lxy \to \forall x \, \forall y \, Lxy)$" from the sentence "$(\exists y \, Lay \to \forall x \, \forall y \, Lxy)$," since the variable "$x$" occurs in the latter. But they do allow us to form the astounding "$\forall z \, (\exists y \, Lzy \to \forall x \, \forall y \, Lxy)$."

"*y*," in the inference from line 6 to line 7. Since all variables range over the same domain, anything allowable as an instance of one variable is allowable as an instance of any other, in UI.

To underline the fact that all variables have the same domain, we write the consequent of the conditional in the premise as "$\forall z \, Lyz$" in the next example, instead of "$\forall y \, Lyx$."

4.8   EXAMPLE: ALMA INFLAMED BY HER OWN NARCISSISM

All love all lovers.
Alma loves herself.
───────────────
Alma loves the Baron.

1	$\forall x \, (\exists y \, Lxy \rightarrow \forall z \, Lzx)$	(premise)
2	Laa	(premise)
3	$\neg \, Lab$	($\neg$ conclusion)
4	$\checkmark \, (\exists y \, Lay \rightarrow \forall z \, Lza)$	(from 1)
5	$\checkmark \, (\exists y \, Lby \rightarrow \forall z \, Lzb)$	(from 1)

6   $\checkmark \, \neg \exists y \, Lay$ $\forall z \, Lza$ (from 4)
7   $\forall y \, \neg \, Lay$ (from 6)
8   $\neg \, Laa$ (from 7)
×

9   $\checkmark \, \neg \exists y \, Lby$ $\forall z \, Lzb$ (from 5)
10   $\forall y \, \neg \, Lby$ Lab (from 9)
11   $\neg \, Lba$ ×   (from 10)
12   Lba (from 6)
×

4.9   *AMOR VINCIT OMNIA*

All love all lovers.
───────────────
If anyone loves, all love all.

1	$\forall x\,(\exists y\ Lxy \to \forall y\ Lyx)$	(premise)
2	$\checkmark\ \neg(\exists x\ \exists y\ Lxy \to \forall x\ \forall y\ Lxy)$	($\neg$ conclusion)
3	$\checkmark\ \exists x\ \exists y\ Lxy$	(from 2)
4	$\checkmark\ \neg\forall x\ \forall y\ Lxy$	(from 2)
5	$\checkmark\ \exists y\ Lay$	(from 3)
6	Lab	(from 5)
7	$\checkmark\ \exists x\ \neg\forall y\ Lxy$	(from 4)
8	$\checkmark\ \neg\forall y\ Lcy$	(from 7)
9	$\checkmark\ \exists y\ \neg Lcy$	(from 8)
10	$\neg Lcd$	(from 9)
11	$\checkmark\ (\exists y\ Lay \to \forall y\ Lya)$	(from 1)

12	$\checkmark\ \neg\exists y\ Lay$	$\forall y\ Lya$	(from 11)
13	$\forall y\ \neg Lay$		(from 12)
14	$\neg Lab$		(from 13)
	×		
15		$\checkmark\ (\exists y\ Ldy \to \forall y\ Lyd)$	(from 1)
16	$\checkmark\ \neg\exists y\ Ldy$	$\forall y\ Lyd$	(from 15)
17	$\forall y\ \neg Ldy$	Lcd	(from 16)
18	$\neg Lda$	×	(from 17)
19	Lda		(from 12)
	×		

4.10 PROBLEMS

Use the tree method throughout. There are partial solutions at the end of the book.

1. Is this argument valid? "All love all lovers, so Alma loves the Baron, for he loves her." (Conclusion: "Lab.")

2. Is "All love all" a logical truth?

3. Is this sentence consistent? "There is someone who shaves exactly those people who do not shave themselves": $\exists x\ \forall y\ (Sxy \leftrightarrow \neg Syy)$.

4. Is this argument valid? "Holmes can trap himself, for anyone can trap him who can trap everyone he can": $\forall x\ [\forall y\ (Tay \to Txy) \to Txa]$, so Taa.

5. Is this argument valid? "Alma has a brother who has no brother, so she's no one's brother": $\exists x\ (Bxa \land \forall y\ \neg Byx)$, so $\forall x\ \neg Bax$.

6. Is this argument valid? "Alma is an only child, for she loves no one, and only only children love only only children." Conclusion: "*Oa*." The second premise says that $\forall x \, [\forall y \, (Lxy \to Oy) \to Ox]$.

7. Is this argument valid? "Anyone's a sage who's as old as a sage, and Methuselah is as old as anyone, so he's a sage if anyone is": $\exists x \, Sx \to Sa$, since $\forall x \, [\exists y \, (Sy \wedge Oxy) \to Sx]$ and $\forall x \, Oax$.

8. Is this argument valid? "All circles are figures, so all who draw circles draw figures": $\forall x \, (Cx \to Fx)$, so $\forall x \, [\exists y \, (Cy \wedge Dxy) \to \exists y \, (Fy \wedge Dxy)]$.

9. Are the following two sentences logically equivalent?

(i) $\forall x \, (\exists y \, Lxy \to \forall y \, Lyx)$ (ii) $\forall x \, \forall y \, \forall z \, (Lxy \to Lzx)$

10. (*a*) Do sentences (i) and (ii) together form a consistent set?

(i) $\forall x \, [\exists y \, (Lxy \wedge Lya) \to \neg \, Lxa]$ (ii) *Laa*

(*b*) If (ii) means that Alma loves herself, what does (i) mean?

4.11 INFINITE COUNTEREXAMPLES

In Chapter 3 the tree test always terminates after some finite number of passes from stage 6 back up to stage 2 in the flow graph of Figure 3.1. But now that we have other quantifiers besides "$\forall x$" and "$\exists x$," using other variables, rule 6 of formation allows the sort of nesting found in the sentence "$\forall x \, \exists y \, Mxy$," which has this formation tree:

$$(0) \qquad Mab$$
$$|$$
$$(6) \qquad \exists y \, May$$
$$|$$
$$(6) \qquad \forall x \, \exists y \, Mxy$$

Such nesting can lead to endlessly growing trees. To see how, let's test validity of the obviously invalid argument

$\forall x \, \exists y \, Mxy$	Everyone is a mother.
Maa	Alma is her own mother.

Here are the first 8 lines of the tree:

1	$\forall x \, \exists y \, Mxy$	(premise)
2	$\neg \, Maa$	($\neg$ conclusion)
3	$\checkmark \, \exists y \, May$	(from 1—by UI)
4	Mab	(from 3—by EI, using a new name "*b*")
5	$\checkmark \, \exists y \, Mby$	(from 1—by UI)
6	Mbc	(from 5—by EI, using a new name "*c*")
7	$\checkmark \, \exists y \, Mcy$	(from 1—by UI)
8	Mcd	(from 7—by EI, using a new name "*d*")
etc.		

an interpretation (*C*, end of Section 3.11) in which all its lines are true—including the initial list, which is therefore consistent.

It remains only to verify that if the tree never stops growing, some particular path must never stop growing: there must be a way to follow its development, taking one fork or another whenever it branches, so that we never come to an "×." That's not to say that we can foresee what choices will avoid a dead end, but that there is such a sequence of choices, even if it's only by incredible luck that we might make all of them correctly.

The fact that there will always be such a sequence of choices is an immediate consequence of:

> **König's lemma.** A tree can't grow forever just by getting wider and wider, if each line has only a finite number of immediate descendants; it's got to have at least one branch that grows forever.

Proof. Let's speak in terms of family trees, with each line being the head of the family consisting of its immediate descendants (lines just below it, if any), together with theirs, and so on. Call a line "fit" (as in the phrase "survival of the fit") if the family it heads is infinite, never coming to a dead (×) end, and call it "unfit" if the family it heads is finite. Since each line has only a finite number of immediate descendants: *A line is unfit if each immediate descendant is unfit.* Or, putting it the other way around: *A fit line has at least one fit immediate descendant.*

Now suppose infinite a tree in which each line has only a finite number of immediate descendants. To prove König's lemma we specify a path through that tree, and prove that it has no last line. Of course, the first line of the path is the top line of the tree—a line that is fit by hypothesis, as the tree is infinite. Being fit, that line has at least one fit immediate descendant. Let the second line in the path be the leftmost of these. Since that line is fit, too, it will also have a fit immediate descendant. And so on. At every stage in following this path we can take one more step, as a fit line always has at least one fit immediate descendant—and finitely many, so that there will surely be a leftmost. Then the path never ends.

4.16 TRANSLATION DRILL

With "*Lxy*" for "*x* loathes *y*," correspondences between English and logical notation are illustrated below. Try your hand by covering the right-hand side and translating into logical notation, and by covering the left-hand side and translating the logical notation into English.

We cycle endlessly round the big loop in Figure 3.1, generating new lines by the UI–EI two-step, which for every even $n = 2, 4, 6, \ldots$ adds a pair of new lines:

$n + 1$	$\checkmark\ \exists y\ M\ old\ y$	(from 1—by UI)
$n + 2$	$M\ old\ new$	(from $n + 1$—by EI)

in which the second contains a new name that yields the first line of the next pair by universal instantiation of line 1.

Cycling forever round the flow graph, the program never reaches either stop box and never delivers either verdict—"valid" or "invalid." Of course, in so simple a case as this we easily see that the test will never terminate, and clearly foresee the shape of the unfolding infinite open path. In particular, we see that under the interpretation given in the English version of the argument, the even-numbered lines tell an endless genealogical tale that begins as follows:

2	$\neg\, Maa$	Alma is not her own mother,
4	Mab	but she is Bernice's mother,
6	Mbc	who is Clara's mother,
8	Mcd	who is Dorothy's mother,
etc.		

Observe that although infinitely many different names appear in the story, there's no guarantee that there are infinitely many different bearers of those names. Indeed, there might be only two bearers: Alma, who isn't her own mother, and someone else, a certain Bernice, who has no end of aliases ("Clara," "Dorothy,"...), and who is her own mother. Of course that's impossible, but that's a matter of biology, not logic.

If we interpret these names and the predicate "*M*" in numerical terms as illustrated in Section 3.11, the bearers of the names "*a*," "*b*," "*c*," etc., will be the successive positive integers 1, 2, 3, etc., without end, which together make up the domain of the variables, i.e., an infinite set. And the extension of the predicate letter "*M*" will be the set of pairs $\{(1, 2), (2, 3), (3, 4), \ldots\}$, since "*Mab*," "*Mbc*," "*Mcd*," ... are the atomic sentences appearing as lines of the tree. Then on this interpretation, "*Mxy*" means that $x + 1 = y$.

The program never generates the whole story, but that's a matter of physics, not logic. So far as mere logic goes, the first pass round the loop in Figure 3.1 might take half a minute, the second might take a quarter, the third an eighth, and in general the $n + 1$st pass might take just half as long as the *n*th, so that after a full minute the whole infinite story would have been told—even though at any time short of the full minute only a finite

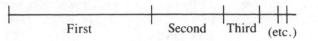

FIGURE 4.5
Son of Zeno.

initial fragment had been told (see Figure 4.5, where each step covers half the remaining distance to the right-hand end, which is approached as closely as you please by taking a large enough finite number of steps, but could be reached only by taking an infinity of steps).

4.12   MORE PROBLEMS

Use the tree test. As in Section 3.11, describe interpretations determined by open paths through trees in Problems 1–3. There are partial solutions at the end of the book.

1. Is this argument valid? "Everyone loves Alma, so someone loves everyone":
   $\forall x\ Lxa$, so $\exists x\ \forall y\ Lxy$.
2. Which are logical truths? (Which have inconsistent denials?)
   (a) $\forall x\ (Px \to \forall y\ Py)$ (b) $\exists x\ (Px \to \exists y\ Py)$
   (c) $\forall x\ (Px \to \exists y\ Py)$ (d) $\exists x\ (Px \to \forall y\ Py)$
3. Are (i) and (ii) logically equivalent; i.e., do they imply each other?
   (i) $\exists x\ \forall y\ Lyx$ (ii) $\forall x\ \exists y\ Lxy$
4. Are (i) and (ii) logically equivalent?
   (i) At each stage some path is open: $\forall x\ [Sx \to \exists y\ (Py\ \wedge\ Oyx)]$
   (ii) There's a path that never closes: $\exists y\ [Py\ \wedge\ \forall x\ (Sx \to Oyx)]$

4.13   UNDECIDABILITY

In the presence of multiple generality the tree test is no longer a decision procedure; a finite set of sentences can be consistent but escape detection by the tree test, which cycles on forever round the loop in the flow graph of Figure 3.1 without making a judgment (see Section 4.11). Too bad—but as we'll see in Chapter 8, that's a limitation not only of the tree test but of any systematic consistency test that's sound and complete, i.e. trustworthy with regard to both possible answers. Meanwhile, let's establish that any answers the tree test does give are still trustworthy, now that trees can be infinite.

4.14   SOUNDNESS

In Section 3.15 we could state the soundness theorem so: "If the initial list is consistent, there's an open path through the finished tree." But now, to

---

cover the possibility that the tree is one that grows forever, we must put it a bit differently:

> If the initial list is consistent, there will be an open path through each finished or unfinished tree obtainable from it by the rules of inference.

For trees that eventually stop growing, this comes to the same thing as the earlier formulation, but it also applies to infinite trees.

If there is an interpretation in which all of a path's lines are true, no line can be the denial of another; the path must be open. Then to prove the soundness theorem, we need prove only this:

> **Soundness lemma.** If (1) all lines of a path are true in an interpretation and (2) the path is extended (and perhaps split) by applying a rule of inference to one of its lines, then (3) all lines of at least one of the extended paths are true in some interpretation.

Proof. If the rule of inference in (2) is sound, all lines of one of the extended paths will be true in the same interpretation in which all lines of the unextended path were true. That covers all but the unsound rule EI, which adds a single line $...n...$ at the bottom of the path when we check the line $\exists x...x...$ (or $\exists y...y...$, etc.), n being a new name. Now if all lines of the unextended path are true in an interpretation that assigns extensions to one or more names that don't appear in the path, all will still be true if we trim the interpretation by dropping extensions of such extraneous names, which can't affect the truth values of sentences in the path. Call that trimmed interpretation "C." By hypothesis the line $\exists x...x...$ of the unextended path is true in C, so the thing that $\exists x...x...$ says is true of some x must be true of some individual i in the domain that C assigns to the variables. Let's modify C by assigning i as extension to the name n that appears in the new line $...n....$ Call that modification "C_i." If all lines of the original path are true in C, all those, and the new line as well, will be true in C_i.

4.15   COMPLETENESS

> The initial list is consistent if there is an open path through each finished or unfinished tree obtainable from it by following the flow graph (Figure 3.1).

If the tree eventually stops growing, the antecedent of this conditional says that there is an open path through the finished tree. Such a path determines

Loathing

1. The Baron is loathed by Alma. Lab
2. The Baron loathes Alma. Lba
3. Alma and the Baron loathe each other. $(Lab \wedge Lba)$
4. The Count loathes the Baron if Alma does. $(Lab \to Lcb)$
5. The Count loathes the Baron only if Alma does. $(Lcb \to Lab)$
6. The Count loathes the Baron if and only if Alma does. $(Lcb \leftrightarrow Lab)$
7. Alma loathes someone. $\exists y\, Lay$
8. Someone loathes Alma. $\exists y\, Lya$
9. Alma loathes everyone. $\forall y\, Lay$
10. Everyone loathes Alma. $\forall y\, Lya$
11. Alma loathes no one. $\neg \exists y\, Lay;\ \forall y\, \neg Lay$
12. No one loathes Alma. $\neg \exists y\, Lya;\ \forall y\, \neg Lya$
13. Alma doesn't loathe everyone. $\neg \forall y\, Lay;\ \exists y\, \neg Lay$
14. Not everyone loathes Alma. $\neg \forall y\, Lya;\ \exists y\, \neg Lya$
15. The Count loathes everyone whom Alma loathes. $\forall y\, (Lay \to Lcy)$
16. The Count loathes someone whom Alma loathes. $\exists y\, (Lay \wedge Lcy)$
17. The Count loathes everyone who loathes Alma. $\forall y\, (Lya \to Lcy)$
18. The Count loathes someone who loathes Alma. $\exists y\, (Lcy \wedge Lya)$
19. The Count loathes some who loathe themselves. $\exists y\, (Lcy \wedge Lyy)$
20. The Count loathes all who loathe themselves. $\forall y\, (Lyy \to Lcy)$
21. The Count loathes only those who loathe themselves. $\forall y\, (Lcy \to Lyy)$
22. All who loathe themselves loathe the Count. $\forall y\, (Lyy \to Lyc)$
23. Some who loathe themselves loathe the Count. $\exists y\, (Lyy \wedge Lyc)$
24. All who loathe themselves loathe everyone. $\forall y\, (Lyy \to \forall z\, Lyz)$
25. Some who loathe themselves loathe everyone. $\exists y\, (Lyy \wedge \forall z\, Lyz)$
26. Some are loathed by everyone they loathe. $\exists x\, \forall y\, (Lxy \to Lyx)$

Fear and Loathing

27. Alma fears and loathes the Baron. $(Fab \wedge Lab)$
28. Alma fears everyone she loathes. $\forall y\, (Lay \to Fay)$
29. Some fear everyone they loathe. $\exists x\, \forall y\, (Lxy \to Fxy)$
30. All fear everyone they loathe. $\forall x\, \forall y\, (Lxy \to Fxy)$
31. Alma fears everybody. $\forall y\, Fay$
32. Someone fears everybody. $\exists x\, \forall y\, Fxy$
33. Alma is feared by someone. $\exists y\, Fya$

34. Everybody is feared by someone. $\forall x\, \exists y\, Fyx$

35. Achilles is a Trojan; Achilles is a Greek. $Ta;\ Ga$

36. Achilles is a Trojan who fears all Greeks. $Ta\ \wedge\ \forall y\, (Gy \rightarrow Fay)$

37. Each Greek is feared by some Trojan. $\forall x\, [Gx \rightarrow \exists y\, (Ty\ \wedge\ Fyx)]$

4.17 EXERCISES

There are translations at the back of the book for problems 1 and 2.

1. Test the validity of the following argument, using the tree method:

(a) Some Trojan is feared by all Greeks.

(b) Each Greek fears some Trojan.

2. Test the validity of the following argument, using the tree method:

(a) Any fearless Greek loathes all Trojans.

(b) There's at least one Trojan.

(c) Every Greek who loathes a Trojan is feared by all.

(d) Achilles loathes a Trojan.

(e) If Achilles is Greek, everyone fears him.

3. Translate into logical notation, using "Kxy" for x knows y, "a" for Alma.

(a) Some know all.

(b) Some know all who know Alma.

(c) Some know all who know them.

(d) Some know all who know themselves.

(e) Some who know themselves know Alma.

(f) All who know Alma know themselves.

(g) All who know all know some who know Alma.

(h) Anyone who knows everyone Alma knows knows Alma.

(i) No one who knows anyone Alma knows knows everyone Alma knows.

(j) Everyone who knows everyone Alma knows knows someone who knows Alma.

5

IDENTITY

The sign " = " of identity is a two-place predicate like "loves"; in both cases (mathspeak, English) we can form sentences by writing the sign between two names or between two occurrences of the same name. But although the predicate "loves" ("L," in logical notation) can hold only in rather special domains, the identity predicate " = " (or "I," in logical notation) can hold in every domain; and while general truths about loving are elusive, general truths about identity are readily formulated, e.g., these two:

1. Everything is identical with itself. $\qquad\qquad\qquad\qquad \forall x\ Ixx$

2. What's true of a thing is true of what's identical with it.

$$\forall x\ \forall y\ [(Px \land Ixy) \to Py]$$

We won't insist on the "I" notation; we shall also use the familiar notation in which " = " is written between variables:

1. $\forall x\ x = x$ $\qquad\qquad\qquad$ **2.** $\forall x\ \forall y\ [(Px \land x = y) \to Py]$

5.1 RULES OF INFERENCE FOR IDENTITY

Instead of adopting laws like (1) and (2) above as axioms for identity, we add rules of inference that make the tree method deliver them as logical truths.

Here is the tree that must close if "$\forall x\, Ixx$" is to be delivered. It's shown in both notations—"I" on the left and "$=$" in the middle and again at the right, where we illustrate the use of the stroke "$/$" through the sign "$=$" as an alternative sign of denial.

$$\checkmark \neg \forall x\, Ixx \qquad \checkmark \neg \forall x\, x = x \qquad \checkmark \neg \forall x\, x = x$$
$$\checkmark \exists x\, \neg Ixx \qquad \checkmark \exists x\, \neg x = x \qquad \checkmark \exists x\, x \neq x$$
$$\neg Iaa \qquad\qquad \neg a = a \qquad\qquad a \neq a$$

The tree is still open. To make it close, we add the following rule for *diversity* $\neq$, a rule for denied identity sentences. Illustrated here for the name "a," it's intended for all other names as well.

$\neg$ Identity. Close paths containing lines "$\neg Iaa$" (or "$a \neq a$").

$$\frac{a \neq a}{\times}$$

We'll also need a rule for undenied identity. To see what it must be, let's consider an argument that will be valid according to the principle (2) that what's true of a thing is true of what's identical with it. Here things are places—where Min lives (a) and works (b)—and what's true of them is that Min isn't there ($\neg Ma$) or that she is (Mb).

Min is home or at work.	$Ma \lor Mb$
She's not home.	$\neg Ma$

She doesn't work at home.	$\neg a = b$

(The conclusion is that Min's home $\neq$ Min's workplace.) The tree needs to close:

1	$\checkmark Ma \lor Mb$	(premise)
2	$\neg Ma$	(premise)
3	$\checkmark \neg\neg a = b$	($\neg$ conclusion)
4	$Ma \qquad Mb$	(from 1)
5	$\times \qquad a = b$	(from 3)
6	$?$	(from ??)
	$\times$	

It will; a new, two-premise rule for undenied identity (with "*a*" and "*b*" as sample names) yields a sixth line "?" that closes the tree.

Identity. If an open path has a line (1) "$a = b$" and a line (2) in which one of those names appears, write at the bottom a line like (2) but with the other name at one or more of those places—unless that's already a line of the path. *Don't check either premise.*

$$
\begin{array}{cc}
a = b & a = b \\
\ldots a \ldots & \ldots b \ldots \\
\hline
\ldots b \ldots & \ldots a \ldots
\end{array}
$$

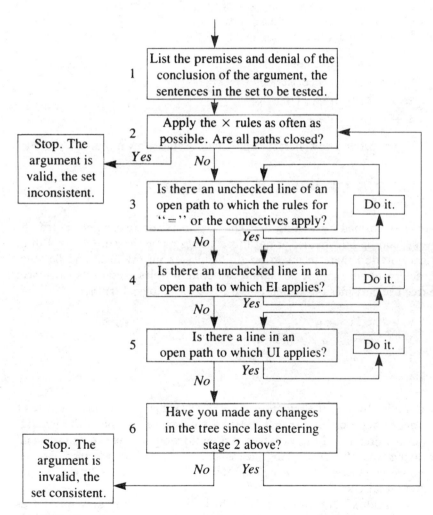

FIGURE 5.1
Flowchart for rules of inference.

Line 5 of the right-hand path is "$a = b$," and the path has lines of forms $\ldots a \ldots$ (line 2, "$\neg Ma$") and $\ldots b \ldots$ (line 4, "Mb"). Then we can make either of two moves at line 6 to close the path. Since "$a = b$" and "$\neg Ma$" are full lines, we can replace the question mark by "$\neg Mb$," which closes the path because it's the denial of line 4. Or, since "$a = b$" and "Mb" are full lines, we can replace the question mark by "Ma," which closes the path because it's the denial of line 2. Here are the alternative line 6's:

6    $\neg Mb$ (from 5, 2)   6 Ma (from 5, 4)
         ×   ×

Another example. The following test of the valid inference from "$a = b$" to "$b = a$" uses both the new rules: *identity* to get line 3 from lines 1 and 2, and $\neg$ *identity* to get line 4 from line 3, closing the tree:

1    $a = b$ (premise)
2    $b \neq a$ ($\neg$ conclusion)
3    $a \neq a$ (from 1 and 2)
4   ×   (from 3)

Figure 5.1 is a flowchart for applying the rules now at hand.

5.2 SAYING OF WHAT IS NOT THAT IT IS NOT

A sentence formed by writing the sign "$=$" between two names is true or false depending on whether or not those names name the same thing. But in logical notation there seems to be a difficulty about mythical and fictional characters, for in naming something we commit ourselves to its existence; the tree test classifies the sentence "$\exists x\ x = a$" as a logical truth:

1    $\checkmark \neg \exists x\ x = a$
2    $\forall x \neg x = a$ (from 1)
3    $\neg a = a$ (from 2)
4   ×   (from 3)

Then if a is Holmes, the sentence "$\exists x\ x = a$" (Some x is Holmes) is true or false depending on whether or not Holmes exists, i.e., is one of the individuals in the domain of the variables, a domain we may take to comprise all the living and the dead. This means that when asked whether Holmes exists, we can't consistently answer "No," for the sentence "$\neg \exists x\ x = a$" is a logical falsehood.

A paradox? No, just a confusion. If there isn't any such person as Holmes, it makes no sense to talk about giving Holmes a name. We'd better talk about the name "Holmes," and ask whether it has a bearer. There's no paradox in answering "no" to that. If the name "Holmes" has no bearer, this will be true:

> There's no interpretation in which the extension of "a" is the bearer of the name "Holmes."

That's why we can't translate "Holmes doesn't exist" into logical notation as "$\neg \exists x \ x = a$." But we can translate it into a sentence *about* logical notation—the sentence displayed above.

5.3 DEFINITE DESCRIPTIONS

In various examples we have evaluated arguments about Holmes and other fictional characters—for the fun of it. Taken with obvious grains of salt, that served well enough to illustrate sober uses of logic where names have referents. But in scientific talk, too, there may be doubt about the existence of putative entities under discussion.

Before 1930 someone might have speculated about the existence of a planet more remote than Neptune, and provisionally assigned it the name "Pluto." The sentence "Pluto is less massive than the Earth" was not then known to be true or, indeed, to be a suitable vehicle for statement making. The sentence purports to refer to the one and only one planet that's more remote than Neptune—if such there be. Assuming that there is exactly one such thing, we want to be understood as saying that it is less massive than the Earth, but if there is not one such thing, we are prepared to admit that the presupposition was false, on the basis of which we proposed to use the word "Pluto." Then the needs of communication can be met by saying:

1. There is exactly one planet more remote than Neptune, and that planet is less massive than the Earth

instead of the shorter but trickier:

2. Pluto is less massive than the Earth.

Sentence 2 is tricky in concealing a possibly false assumption, an assumption that's made quite explicit in sentence 1. Because it makes no use of the questionable name "Pluto," 1 must be more explicit than 2; it must explicitly state the assumption that 2 masks by using the name "Pluto." Then if "a" names Pluto, if "Lx" means that x is less massive than the Earth, and if "Mx" means that x is a planet more remote than Neptune, "Pluto is less massive than the Earth" becomes "La" while the more explicit sentence 1 goes over into logical notation more elaborately, as

3. $\exists x \ [Mx \ \wedge \ \forall y \ (My \to y = x) \ \wedge \ Lx]$

where the questionable name "a" does not occur. The first two conjuncts in the brackets of line 3 express the presupposition that there is one and only one planet more remote than Neptune: "Mx" says that x is one, and "$\forall y\,(My \rightarrow y = x)$" says that any other, y, is in fact x itself (perhaps under another name). Finally, the third conjunct says that this unique x is less massive than the Earth, and it says this only after the assumptions about x that are implicit in calling it "Pluto" have been made explicit.

5.4 NUMBER

One of the characteristic uses of the sign of identity is to say how many things there are that meet a certain description. Of course we can say that at least one thing has the property P without using the sign "$=$":

There is at least 1 P. $\exists x\ Px$

But to say that there is exactly one thing with the property P we must use the sign "$=$":

There is exactly 1 P. $\exists x\,[Px \,\wedge\, \forall y\,(Py \rightarrow y = x)]$

This breaks up into:

There is at least 1 P and at most 1 P.

    $\exists x\,[Px$ $\wedge\ \forall y\,(Py \rightarrow y = x)]$

Similarly we can say that there are at least 2 P's:

There are at least 2 P's. $\exists x\,\exists y\,(Px \,\wedge\, Py \,\wedge\, x \neq y)$

(It is essential that we specify that x and y are distinct, "$x \neq y$," for distinct variables need not represent distinct individuals.) Now to say that there are exactly two P's we can say that there are at least two, $\exists x\,\exists y\,[Px \,\wedge\, Py \,\wedge\, x \neq y \ldots$, and that's all, i.e., any z that's a P is one of the aforementioned: $\ldots \wedge \forall z\,[Pz \rightarrow (z = x \,\vee\, z = y)]\}$.

There are exactly 2 P's. $\exists x\,\exists y\,\{Px \,\wedge\, Py \,\wedge\, x \neq y \,\wedge\, \forall z\,[Pz \rightarrow (z = x \,\vee\, z = y)]\}$

      To say that there are exactly n P's, we say that there are at least n, and no more. But when n is 3 or more, the statement that there are at least n P's requires an unexpectedly large number of disclaimers of identity, because x can be different from y and y can be different from z when x and z are the same, e.g., if $x = z = $ Min, and $y = $ Henry.

There are at least 3 P's. $\exists x \,\exists y \,\exists z \,(x \neq y \,\wedge\, x \neq z \,\wedge\, y \neq z \,\wedge\, Px \,\wedge\, Py \,\wedge\, Pz)$

There are at least 4 P's. $\exists x \,\exists y \,\exists z \,\exists w \,(x \neq y \,\wedge\, x \neq z \,\wedge\, x \neq w \,\wedge\, y \neq z$

$\wedge\, y \neq w \,\wedge\, z \neq w \,\wedge\, Px \,\wedge\, Py \,\wedge\, Pz \,\wedge\, Pw)$

5.5 PROBLEMS

Use the tree method. (There's a partial solution to 3 in Section 5.9.)

1. Test validity of the following arguments:
   (a) "$a = b$, so $Pa \rightarrow Pb$"
   (b) "$Pa \leftrightarrow Pb$, so $a = b$"

2. Show that the following are logical truths about identity:
   (a) *Reflexivity.* $\forall x \; x = x$
   (b) *Symmetry.* $\forall x \,\forall y \,(x = y \rightarrow y = x)$
   (c) *Transitivity.* $\forall x \,\forall y \,\forall z \,[(x = y \,\wedge\, y = z) \rightarrow x = z]$

3. *Diversity.* Which parts (*a* to *c*) of problem 2 remain logical truths when all signs " = " of identity are replaced by signs " ≠ " of diversity?

4. *Monotheism.* Test validity of the following argument:

   There's at least one God. $\exists x \; Gx$

   There's at most one. $\forall x \,\forall y \,[(Gx \,\wedge\, Gy) \rightarrow x = y]$

   There's exactly one. $\exists x \,[Gx \,\wedge\, \forall y \,(Gy \rightarrow x = y)]$

5. *Logical equivalence.* Show that "$\exists x \,\forall y \,(Gy \leftrightarrow x = y)$" is another way of saying that there's exactly one God.

6. *Logical equivalence.* Show that "$\forall x \,\forall y \,\forall z \,\exists w \,(Pw \,\wedge\, w \neq x \,\wedge\, w \neq y \,\wedge\, w \neq z)$" is another way of saying that there are at least 4 P's. (This tree is extremely nasty if you do useless UIs.)

7. By the tree method, prove that the following four ways of saying that the president is queasy are logically equivalent. *Note:* It's enough to test validity of a cycle of four arguments.
   (a) $\exists x \,(Px \,\wedge\, Qx) \,\wedge\, \forall x \,\forall y \,[(Px \,\wedge\, Py) \rightarrow x = y]$
   (b) $\forall x \,(Px \rightarrow Qx) \,\wedge\, \exists x \,\forall y \,(Py \leftrightarrow y = x)$
   (c) $\exists x \,[Px \,\wedge\, Qx \,\wedge\, \forall y \,(Py \rightarrow y = x)]$
   (d) $\exists x \,[Qx \,\wedge\, \forall y \,(Py \leftrightarrow y = x)]$

5.6 RULE OF INTERPRETATION FOR IDENTITY

The extension assigned to the identity predicate "I" (or " $=$ ") in an interpretation is completely determined by the domain that interpretation assigns to the variables. Since each individual is identical with itself, and with nothing else, that extension is the set containing all pairs (i, i) where i is a member of the domain, and containing nothing else.

5.7 SOUNDNESS

The rules of inference for identity and diversity are both sound. *Diversity:* the one-premise rule directing us to close paths containing lines that deny self-identity can't lead from a premise that's true in an interpretation to a conclusion that's false in that interpretation, because in all interpretations self-identity sentences are true, and their denials false. *Identity*: the result of substituting equals for equals must be true in any interpretation in which both premises are true.

Since the new rules for I and $\neg I$ (for $=$ and $\neq$) are both sound, the soundness of the tree test proved in Section 4.15 is preserved when identity is added to our notation.

5.8 COMPLETENESS

> If some path never closes, the initial list is consistent.

For trees without identity we proved this (Sections 3.14 and 4.15) by observing that all rules of inference—even UI—have the property of *path completeness*, defined (Section 3.11) in terms of the particular interpretations C determined by sets of quantifier-free lines appearing in open paths through finished trees. A rule of inference is path-complete iff the following is true of every never-closing path in every tree: *if all lines that come from a given line via the rule are true in* C, *so is that line.*

Now to prove completeness of the tree method as extended to identity, we modify the definition of C and verify that all the rules of inference are path-complete by that definition. As in Section 3.11, this new definition of C is designed to inject truth or falsity into atomic sentences, depending on whether or not they appear as full lines of the path, and to define C's domain and the extensions it assigns to names and predicate letters in such a way as to draw truth-in-C up from full lines to the lines they come from via rules of inference.

In the case of the complete rules—all but UI and, now, the rule for identity—any consistent definition of C would have done, but to ensure path-completeness of the incomplete rule UI in Chapter 3 and 4, we had to choose C's domain as the set of all extensions of names that appear in the path (Section 3.11). Continuing to take C's domain to consist of the extensions it assigns to names, we now modify those assignments in order to make the rule for identity path-complete, without disturbing the path-completeness of UI.

In Section 3.11 the extensions of names in order of appearance in the path—their "old extensions"—were the successive positive integers in order of magnitude. But if an identity statement is a full line of the path, we want the two names flanking " $=$ " (or following " I ") to have the same new extension. To accomplish that we divide the names that appear in any open, finished path into classes, where names—say, "a" and "b"—belong to the same class if and only if the sentence "$a = b$" appears in the path as a full line. The modified interpretation C that's determined by the open path assigns to all names in the same class the smallest number that's the old extension of any of them.

5.9 EXAMPLES OF MODIFIED INTERPRETATIONS

Example 1. The sentence "$\forall x\ \forall y\ \forall z\ [(x \neq y \wedge y \neq z) \rightarrow x \neq z]$" is not a logical truth; the tree starting with its denial consists of a single open path in which the names "a," "b," and "c" appear, in that order, and in which the relevant quantifier-free full lines are the following:

$$
\begin{array}{cl}
7 & \checkmark \neg [(a \neq b \wedge b \neq c) \rightarrow a \neq c] \\
10 & a \neq b \\
11 & b \neq c \\
12 & a = c
\end{array}
$$

The old extensions of "a," "b," "c" are 1, 2, 3; line 12 gives "a" and "c" the same new extension, i.e., the old extension, 1, of "a"; and since no lines are identity sentences connecting "b" to "a" or to "c," "b" retains its old extension, 2. Then C's domain is the set $\{1, 2\}$, and the extensions it assigns to "a," "b," and "c" are 1, 2, and 1, respectively.

Example 2. The consistency test for the sentences in lines 1 through 4 below produces an open finished tree with a single path, beginning as follows, which determines an interpretation C.

$$
\begin{array}{cl}
1 & a \neq b \\
2 & b = c \\
3 & c = d \\
4 & d \neq e
\end{array}
$$

None of the further lines that will appear in the finished path will have any effect on the new extensions of the names "a," "b," "c," "d," "e," whose old extensions are 1, 2, 3, 4, 5, respectively. In view of lines 2 and 3 the names "b," "c," "d" belong to the same class, and each has as its new extension the smallest number that's the old extension of any of them, i.e., 2. But "a" and "e" are alone in their own, separate classes, so that their new extensions are the same as the old. Thus the new extensions of the five names in order of appearance are 1, 2, 2, 2, 5, and the domain of C is the three-membered set $\{1, 2, 5\}$.

5.10 PROBLEMS

By the tree method, test consistency of the sets whose members are listed in 1-4 below. In each case describe the interpretations determined by the open paths: domain, and extensions of all letter names and predicate letters other than "*I*."

1. Brothers and sisters have I none, $\forall x \, (Bbx \to a = x)$, but that man's father is my father's son, Bbc ("*a*" for *me*, "*b*" for *my father*, "*B*" for *begat*).
2. Everybody loves baby, $\forall x \, Lxb$. Baby loves nobody but me, $\forall x \, (Lbx \to a = x)$.
3. $\forall x \, \exists y \, x = y$
4. $\forall x \, \exists y \, x \neq y$
5. *Translation.* Translate the following sentences into the notation of Section 4.16, using "*b*" for Hector. There are answers at the back of the book.
   (*a*) Achilles loathes Hector, and only Hector.
   (*b*) Achilles, and only Achilles, loathes Hector.
   (*c*) Some loathe themselves and only themselves.
   (*d*) Achilles is feared by (all) the Trojans who fear no other Greeks.
   (*e*) Achilles is feared by (some) Trojans who fear no other Greeks.
   (*f*) Achilles is feared by the (one) Trojan who fears no other Greeks.
6. Test validity of the argument from (i) and (ii) by the tree method (translated in the back.)
   (i) Achilles, a Greek, is feared by the Trojans who fear no other Greeks.
   (ii) If every Trojan fears a Greek, all of them fear Achilles.
7. Test consistency of the set {i, ii} by the tree method. In (i), "any" means $\exists$; "all" would have meant $\forall$.
   (i) Greeks who fear any other Greeks loathe themselves.
   (ii) Achilles is a Greek feared by all, loathed by none.
8. "One of every two is ..." is often used as an emphatic way of saying that exactly half are ..., but it's not literally correct. To see why, show by the tree method that both the following arguments are valid. (Their conclusions *don't* follow from the assumptions that at least half and exactly half are female.)
   (*a*) At least one of every two is female, so if anyone isn't, everyone else is.
   (*b*) Exactly one of every two is female, so there are fewer than three.

6

FUNCTIONS

Adam begat Seth, Seth begat Enos, Enos begat Cainan. Writing "Fxy" for "x was the father of y" and "a," "b," "c," "d" for "Adam," "Seth," "Enos," "Cainan," respectively, we can convey the foregoing information so:

$$Fab \qquad Fbc \qquad Fcd$$

But there's another way:

Adam $=$ the father of Seth

Seth $=$ the father of Enos

Enos $=$ the father of Cainan

Introducing a function symbol "f" for "the father of," we can write those in logical notation:

$$a = f(b) \qquad b = f(c) \qquad c = f(d)$$

And we can substitute equals for equals in these, to get

$$a = f(f(c)) \qquad b = f(f(d))$$

i.e., in the vernacular,

Adam $=$ the father of the father of Enos

Seth $=$ the father of the father of Cainan

The thicket of parentheses in "$f(f(f(d)))$" is unnecessary; it's just as clear to write "$fffd$." We'll often write "fa," "fx," etc., instead of "$f(a)$," "$f(x)$," etc.

6.1 RULE OF FORMATION

If the function symbol "f" is to produce a name whenever it is applied to a name, the function must be defined in such a way that there is always exactly one object $f(name)$ corresponding to each named object. Then according to Genesis, *the father of* will not do as an interpretation of the function symbol "f," for if x is Adam or Eve there is no such object as $f(x)$. We might remedy this defect by arbitrarily assigning values to the function f for these two arguments, perhaps as follows:

$$f(x) = \begin{cases} \text{the father of } x, \text{ if } x \text{ has a father} \\ \text{Adam, if } x \text{ has no father.} \end{cases}$$

(The jargon here is the same as in mathematics. Never mind that f's arguments and values aren't numbers but people; its arguments are the entities to which the function f can be applied, i.e., all individuals in the domain of the variables, and its values are the members of that domain that f assigns to those arguments.) Then since Adam had no father, we have $a = fa = ffa = fffa$, etc. These sentences do not mean that Adam was his own father, paternal grandfather, etc., for according to our careful definition, "f" does not simply mean *the father of*. Similarly, *the teacher of* is not an allowable definition of a function symbol, for some have no teacher and some have more than one.

Our general requirement about the interpretation of any function symbol, say, "f," can be put as follows:

$$\forall x \, \exists y \, \forall z \, (fx = z \leftrightarrow y = z)$$

In English: for each x there is one and only one y such that $y = f(x)$. If we view "fa" as a name for purposes of UI (see line 5 below), the tree method will classify that as a logical truth:

1	$\checkmark \, \neg \forall x \, \exists y \, \forall z \, (fx = z \leftrightarrow y = z)$	($\neg$ logical truth)
2	$\checkmark \, \exists x \, \neg \exists y \, \forall z \, (fx = z \leftrightarrow y = z)$	(from 1 by $\neg \forall$)
3	$\checkmark \, \neg \exists y \, \forall z \, (fa = z \leftrightarrow y = z)$	(from 2 by EI)
4	$\forall y \, \neg \forall z \, (fa = z \leftrightarrow y = z)$	(from 3 by $\neg \exists$)
5	$\checkmark \, \neg \forall z \, (fa = z \leftrightarrow fa = z)$	(from 4 by UI: "fa" for "y")
6	$\checkmark \, \exists z \, \neg (fa = z \leftrightarrow fa = z)$	(from 5 by $\neg \forall$)
7	$\checkmark \, \neg (fa = b \leftrightarrow fa = b)$	(from 6 by EI)
8	$fa = b \qquad fa \neq b$	(from 7
9	$fa \neq b \qquad fa = b$	by $\neg \leftrightarrow$)
	$\times \qquad\quad \times$	

As the foregoing proof suggests, a minor adjustment of the rules of formation accommodates the tree method to functions:

Formation. When function symbols are applied to names, names result.

Of course there are functions of more than one argument, e.g., addition and multiplication as functions of 2 or 3 arguments:

$$(x + y) \qquad (x \times y) \qquad (x + y + z) \qquad (x \times y \times z)$$

We continue to use the necessary signs of grouping as parts of those function symbols themselves.

A homelier example is the two-place function symbol "g":

$$g(x, y) = \begin{cases} \text{the first offspring of } x \text{ and } y, \text{ if any} \\ x, \text{ if none} \end{cases}$$

Then if "a," "b," and "c" name Adam, Eve, and Cain, Genesis says that "$g(a, b) = c$" is true and suggests by its silence that "$g(b, c) = b$" is also true. Here parentheses are helpful but not essential. For example, if it is understood that "g" has two places and that "f" and "m" (for "the mother of") each have one place, "$gfcmc$" can be parsed only as "$g(f(c), m(c))$" and can name only Cain, according to Genesis.

6.2   RULE OF INTERPRETATION

When an n-place function symbol is applied to n names, a name results. Corresponding to that rule of formation we have the following rule of interpretation for n-place function symbols "f."

Interpretation. The extension that an interpretation C assigns to "f" must be an n-place function assigning a single individual to each n-tuple of individuals.

These assignments must be made for all individuals i *in the domain*, including those to which C assigns no names, for rule 6 of interpretation for quantifiers (page 51) may require extending C to an interpretation C_i assigning i as extension to a name uninterpreted in C.

Example 1: the identity function. In an interpretation C a one-place function symbol "f" might have as extension the function *id* that assigns to each individual i that individual itself: for each individual i in C's domain, $id(i) = i$.

Example 2: the sum. With the set of all natural numbers as domain, the two-place function symbol "s" is assigned the function *sum* as its extension, where $sum(i, j) = i + j$.

6.3 EI AND UI REVISED

The rules EI and UI, introduced in Section 3.6, are reformulated below to accommodate our broadened concept of name, which now covers expressions like "fa" and "$g(a, b)$" along with letters "a" and "b." In these rules "$...x...$" stands for the result of stripping the initial quantifier from some sentence that begins with "$\forall x$" or "$\exists x$," and "$...n...$" stands for the sentence obtained when all "x"s in that result are replaced by the name n. Of course these rules remain valid when the "x"s are replaced by other variables.

> **Existential instantiation, EI.** Given an unchecked line of form $\exists x ...x...$ in an open path: check it, and inspect every open path it's in for lines of form $...n....$ Where there are none, write $...n...$ at the bottom, n being a *letter* new to the path.

The rule EI is unchanged, except that now we must explicitly require what went without saying in earlier chapters: *the new name* n *must be just a letter, not a new concoction like* "fa" *out of letters and function symbols*. To see why, note that the tree test would mistakenly classify the set consisting of sentences 1 and 2 below as inconsistent, if the new name "ma" were used in EI to get line 3.

No males are mothers.	1	$\forall x (Mx \rightarrow \forall y\ x \neq my)$	
There are males.	2	$\checkmark\ \exists x\ Mx$	
	3	Mma	**NO!** (from 3)
	4	$\checkmark\ Mma \rightarrow \forall y\ ma \neq my$	(from 1)
	5	$\neg Mma \qquad\qquad \forall y\ ma \neq my$	(from 4)
	6	$\times \qquad\qquad\quad ma \neq ma$	(from 5)
		$\times$	

> **Universal instantiation, UI.** Given a line of form $\forall x ...x...$ in an open path: don't check it, but for any name n belonging to the path, write $...n...$ at the bottom unless that is already a line of the path. If no names occur in the path, choose some letter name n and write $...n...$ at the bottom.

In UI, too, we sometimes use new names, i.e., when no names yet appear in paths. Here, where it would be merely cumbersome to use, say, "*fa*" instead of just "*a*," we make the simpler choice: the new name must be a single letter.

In revised UI "belonging to" replaces "appearing in" in the old version (Section 3.6). The names belonging to a path include any letters appearing in it, together with further names built out of those with the aid of function symbols appearing in it. Thus, the names "*fa*," "*ffa*," etc., all belong to paths in which any of them appear; and if "*gafb*" appears in a path, endless concoctions out of '*a*," "*b*," "*f*," and "*g*" belong to it, e.g., "*gfgagfbba*."*

6.4 REGULATING UI, WITH FLOWCHART

Without function symbols the only way trees could grow forever was through the UI-EI two-step illustrated by the following consistency test:

1	$\forall x\, \exists y\, Rxy$	(Consistent?)
2	$\checkmark\, \exists y\, Ray$	(from 1 by UI)
3	Rab	(from 2 by EI)
4	$\checkmark\, \exists y\, Rby$	(from 1 by UI)
5	Rbc	(from 4 by EI)
etc.		

Here the even-numbered lines "$\checkmark\, \exists y\, Ray$," "$\checkmark\, \exists y\, Rby$," etc., yield an endless series of new names "*b*," "*c*," etc. But now that we use function symbols, UI itself can produce no end of new names "*fa*," "*ffa*," "*fffa*," etc., as in the following consistency test:

1	$\forall x\, Pfx$	(Consistent?)
2	Pfa	(from 1 by UI with new "*a*" for "*x*")
3	$Pffa$	(from 1 by UI with old "*fa*" for "*x*")
4	$Pfffa$	(from 1 by UI with old "*ffa*" for "*x*")
etc.		

---

* Restoring punctuation from right to left, this is "$g(fg(a, g(fb, b)), a)$."

With UI unrestricted this would permit bogus consistency tests like the following, with two initial sentences:

1	$\forall x\, Pfx$	
2	$\forall x \neg Px$	
3	Pfa	(from 1 by UI)
4	$Pffa$	(from 1 by UI)
5	$Pfffa$	(from 1 by UI)
etc.		

This test never classifies the set consisting of lines 1 and 2 as inconsistent. It would, if in the "Do it" cycle around box 5 of the flowchart UI were ever applied to line 2 with "fa" for "x," but without some restriction on UI such as the one in Figure 6.1, that need never happen; nothing would rule out endless applications of UI to line 1.

With UI regulated as in Figure 6.1, this last consistency test does terminate correctly, even if we begin with line 1 as before. On our first series of passes around the "Do it" loop for box 5 we are allowed to use only letter names in UI:

1	$\forall x\, Pfx$	
2	$\forall x \neg Px$	
3	Pfa	(from 1 by UI)
4	$\neg Pa$	(from 2 by UI)

Now we exit box 5 by the "No" arrow, box 6 by the "yes" arrow, and boxes 2, 3, 4 by the "No" arrows to start our second series of passes through box 5, with "fa" for "x":

5	$Pffa$	(from 1 by UI)
6	$\neg Pfa$	(from 2 by UI)

Now we exit box 5 by the "No" arrow and box 6 by the "Yes" arrow. In box 2 we close the path and exit by the "Yes" arrow, finding the initial list inconsistent.

6.5 ADEQUACY

Adequacy of the tree method with identity is preserved because in adding function symbols we changed only the flow graph, not the effect of the "Do it" rules. It was to prevent the broadened meaning of "name" from producing such changes that we altered the wording of UI and EI so as to require new names to contain no function symbols; that's why the method remains sound.

 Soundness: If all paths close, the initial list is inconsistent. The key to soundness of the method is the soundness lemma proved in Section 4.14. That is unaffected by the presence of function symbols, which never occur in names introduced by the unsound rule EI.

 Completeness: If some path never closes, the initial list is consistent. Figure 6.1 regulates UI to ensure that all universally quantified lines in

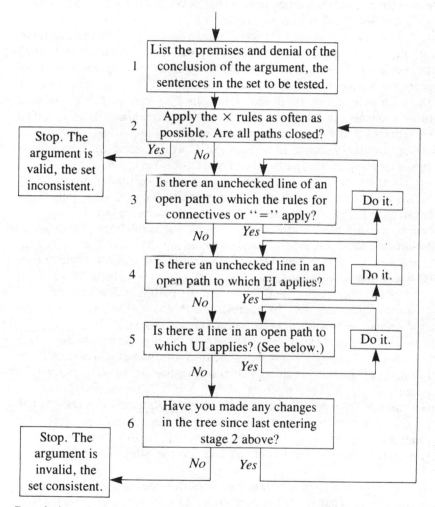

Restriction: during your *n*th trip from box 2 to box 6, apply UI and " = " only with names having fewer than *n* occurrences of function symbols.

FIGURE 6.1

Flowchart for rules of inference.

open paths are instantiated with all names belonging to those paths. Before the introduction of function symbols we got that effect without special regulation. Preserving that feature of the method, regulation preserves completeness of the tree method. To verify that, we need to verify that the rule UI remains path-complete in the presence of function symbols.

Path Completeness. This notion was introduced in Section 3.11, before identity and functions appeared on the scene. To bring it up to date, we now specify particular extensions to be assigned to function symbols by the interpretation C determined by a path that never closes as the tree grows in accordance with the flow graph of Figure 6.1.

Recall that in Section 3.11, before the advent of identity and functions, the domain of C was defined as a set of successive positive integers starting with 1, viz., the extensions of the successive names in the path, in order of appearance. By assuring us that what's true (in C) of all individuals named in the path will be true of all individuals in C's domain, this guaranteed path completeness of UI. When the sign of identity appeared, we modified the extensions that C assigned to names, maintaining path completeness of UI by continuing to define the domain of C as the set of all extensions of names appearing in the path. The modification occurred in Section 5.8, where (in effect) we partitioned the old domain of successive positive integers, assigned to C in Section 4.11, into mutually exclusive, collectively exhaustive cells, where two names belong to the same cell iff they are connected by a chain of identity sentences appearing as full lines of the path in question. We then obtained C's new domain by throwing out all but the smallest number in each cell. The result was still a domain of positive integers, but perhaps with gaps, as when $\{1, 2, 3, 4, 5\}$ reduces to $\{1, 2, 5\}$ because of full lines "$b = c$" and "$d = c$" in the path that determines C.

Now that names may be complex symbols like "fa" and "$g(fa, b)$," the old domain of C will still be an unbroken succession of positive integers, e.g., as when a tree starts with the single line "$fa = b$." (There will be more lines—"$b = b$," "$fa = fa$," "$b = fa$"—but no more names will appear.) The old domain of the interpretation that this four-line path determines will be the set $\{1, 2, 3\}$ of the extensions of "a," "fa," "b," respectively. But the appearance of "$fa = b$" as a full line of this path partitions this set into two cells, the first containing just the number 1, the second containing the number 2 and 3. Dropping 3 from the second cell, we have the new domain, $\{1, 2\}$, where 1 is the extension of "a" and 2 is the extension of "fa" and of "b."

The result is a partial determination of the extension in C of the function symbol "f." That extension is required to be a function—call it "f"—that has a definite value in the domain $\{1, 2\}$ for every argument in that domain. We known that $f(1) = 2$ because in C, 1 is the extension of "a" and 2 is the extension of "fa", but what is the value of $f(2)$? We know that it must be 1 or 2, but nothing in the open path tells us which. What to do?

It doesn't matter. The incompletely specified interpretation C already makes all lines of the path true, so we can set $f(2) = 1$ or 2 as we please. For definiteness, we might agree on 1 as the default setting, i.e., the value that C assigns to functions when the extensions of names in the path don't specify any particular value.

6.6 PROBLEMS

Use the tree method. Describe the interpretations determined by any open paths (solved in the back of the book).

1. Test consistency of "$\forall x\ Pfx$."
2. Test consistency of "$\forall x\ fx = a$."

6.7 MATHEMATICAL REASONING AND GROUPS

Mathematical reasoning is just ordinary reasoning pursued relentlessly, in ways that the vagueness and ambiguity of ordinary premises would make pointless. As a sample, consider the theory of which the axioms are the following three sentences.

G1	$\forall x\ \forall y\ \forall z\ g(x, g(y, z)) = g(g(x, y), z)$
G2	$\forall x\ g(x, a) = x$
G3	$\forall x\ g(x, fx) = a$

This theory (*group theory*) can be interpreted in various ways.

The additive group of the integers: On this interpretation the domain is the set of all the integers, positive, negative, and zero; g is addition, $g(x, y) = x + y$; f is negation, $fx = -x$; and "a" names zero. In a more familiar notation this interpretation of the axioms would be written so:

G1 $\forall x\ \forall y\ \forall z\ [x + (y + z)] = [(x + y) + z]$

G2 $\forall x\ (x + 0) = x$

G3 $\forall x\ (x + -x) = 0$

The multiplicative group of the positive rationals: On this interpretation the domain is the set of all positive rational numbers, ratios i/j where i and j are positive integers. Here a is the number 1, g is multiplication, and f is reciprocation. In G3 below we are to think of "1" and "/" as fused into an indivisible symbol that we interpret as reciprocation.

G1 $\forall x \; \forall y \; \forall z \; [x \times (y \times z)] = [(x \times y) \times z]$

G2 $\forall x \; (x \times 1) = x$

G3 $\forall x \; (x \times 1/x) = 1$

The following cancellation law, G4, is true in every interpretation of axioms G1, G2, G3.

G4 $\forall x \; \forall y \; \forall z \; [g(x, z) = g(y, z) \rightarrow x = y]$

By definition of "valid," this means that the argument from the premises G1, G2, G3 to the conclusion G4 is valid. And by adequacy of the tree test, *this* means that the tree whose initial lines are the axioms and the denial of the conclusion must eventually close. Let's see.

The tree has only one path, but it goes on for some 20 lines. To keep track of the essential moves, we now allow ourselves to cut trivial corners. In the following tree we (1) use the rule for $\neg \forall$ three times to push the denial sign through the block of quantifiers to get from line 4 to line 5, (2) combine three applications of EI to get from line 5 to line 6, and (3) combine three applications of UI, twice, to get from line 1 to lines 9 and 11.

1	$\forall x \; \forall y \; \forall z \; g(x, g(y, z)) = g(g(x, y), z)$	(G1)
2	$\forall x \; g(x, a) = x$	(G2)
3	$\forall x \; g(x, fx) = a$	(G3)
4	$\checkmark \checkmark \checkmark \; \neg \forall x \; \forall y \; \forall z \; [g(x, z) = g(y, z) \rightarrow x = y]$	($\neg$ G4)
5	$\checkmark \checkmark \checkmark \; \exists x \; \exists y \; \exists z \; \neg \, [g(x, z) = g(y, z) \rightarrow x = y]$	(from 4)
6	$\checkmark \neg \, [g(b, d) = g(c, d) \rightarrow b = c]$	(from 5)
7	$g(b, d) = g(c, d)$	(from 6)
8	$b \neq c$	(from 6)
9	$g(b, g(d, fd)) = g(g(b, d), fd)$	(from 1)
10	$g(b, g(d, fd)) = g(g(c, d), fd)$	(from 7, 9)
11	$g(c, g(d, fd)) = g(g(c, d), fd)$	(from 1)
12	$g(d, fd) = a$	(from 3)
13	$g(b, g(d, fd)) = g(c, g(d, fd))$	(from 10, 11)
14	$g(b, a) = g(c, a)$	(from 12, 13)
15	$g(b, a) = b$	(from 2)
16	$g(c, a) = c$	(from 2)
17	$b = g(c, a)$	(from 15, 14)
18	$b = c$	(from 16, 17)
	$\times$	(from 8, 18)

In this 18-line proof we combined steps at some points, but took no serious shortcuts. But now that we've got the hang of the tree test, further pruning can make for clarity. Thus, in the context of group theory there's no point in listing axioms G1, G2, and G3 at the top of every tree, nor need we write the denial of the sentence to be proved as a fourth line; all that can be taken for granted. Nor need we separate the step from line 4 to line 5, (replacing "$\neg \forall x \, \forall y \, \forall z$" by "$\exists x \, \exists y \, \exists z \, \neg$") from the three uses of EI that took us from there to line 6. And we may as well elide the denied conditional line 6, going straight to the two lines (7, 8) we got by checking it. In practice we'd also feel free to combine several applications of the rule for "$=$" noting the lines from which the given line follows, as at 8 below. Then in practice, our 18-line proof might boil down to this:

1	$g(b, d) = g(c, d)$	(from $\neg$ G4)
2	$b \neq c$	(from $\neg$ G4)
3	$g(b, g(d, fd)) = g(g(b, d), fd)$	(from G1)
4	$g(c, g(d, fd)) = g(g(c, d), fd)$	(from G1)
5	$g(d, fd) = a$	(from G3)
6	$g(b, a) = b$	(from G2)
7	$g(c, a) = c$	(from G2)
8	$b = c$	(from 3, 4, 5, 6, 7, 2)
	$\times$	

Highlighted in this short proof are the important choices: which names to use in UI in which axioms once EI has done its work, with a view to substituting equals for equals in a way that closes the path. Routinely following the flow diagram of Figure 6.1, one would eventually make the right instantiations and substitutions—along with many that play no role in closing the path. Such mechanically generated proofs are acceptable, but seeing why they work requires trimming.

Note well: Where function symbols occur, the restriction on UI in Figure 6.1 is essential to establish invalidity; but if you manage to make all paths close, it doesn't matter whether you've respected the restriction on UI.

6.8 PROBLEMS

Using the pruned tree test illustrated in the eight-line proof above, show that G5 follows from G1 through G4 and that G6 follows from G2 and G5. These are solved at the end of the book.

G5 $\forall x \, g(x, a) = g(a, x)$ G6 $\forall y \, [\forall x \, g(x, y) = x \rightarrow y = a]$

By the pruned tree test, show that each of G7 through G10 follows from lower-numbered G's. Don't prune so much that you get lost. These are hard. There are hints at the end of the book for G7 through G9.

G7 $\forall x \ g(x, fx) = g(fx, x)$

G8 $\forall x \ \forall y \ \forall z \ [g(z, x) = g(z, y) \rightarrow x = y]$

G9 $\forall x \ \forall y \ [g(x, y) = a \rightarrow y = fx]$

G10 $\forall x \ ffx = x$

6.9   ROBINSON ARITHMETIC

Sentences Q1 through Q7 below, the axioms of "Robinson arithmetic," are true in the following interpretation.

Domain: the set $N = \{0, 1, 2, \ldots\}$ of all natural numbers.

Extension of "0": the number zero.

Extension of "s": the successor function, $1+$.

Extensions of "$+$" and "$\times$": the functions plus and times.

Q1 $\forall x \ \forall y \ (x \neq y \rightarrow sx \neq sy)$

Q2 $\forall x \ 0 \neq sx$

Q3 $\forall x \ (x \neq 0 \rightarrow \exists y \ x = sy)$

Q4 $\forall x \ (x + 0) = x$

Q5 $\forall x \ \forall y \ (x + sy) = s(x + y)$

Q6 $\forall x \ (x \times 0) = 0$

Q7 $\forall x \ \forall y \ (x \times sy) = [(x \times y) + x]$

The first three of these are general truths about the successor function:

Q1   Distinct natural numbers have distinct successors.

Q2   Zero isn't the successor of a natural number.

Q3   But every other natural number is.

The next two axioms tell us all we need to know about addition in order to add in this notation ("base 1 notation"), where 0, 1, 2, and 10 are written "0," "s0," "ss0," and "sssssssssss0."

Q4   Adding 0 changes nothing.

Q5 $x + (y + 1) = (x + y) + 1$

Here's a pruned tree for the argument "Q4, Q5, so $2 + 2 = 4$." (It closes; the denial of line 5, the conclusion, is an invisible line 0.)

1	$(ss0 + 0) = ss0$	(Q4)
2	$(ss0 + s0) = s(ss0 + 0)$	(Q5)
3	$(ss0 + ss0) = s(ss0 + s0)$	(Q5)
4	$(ss0 + ss0) = ss(ss0 + 0)$	(2, 3)
5	$(ss0 + ss0) = sss s0$	(1, 4)

The last two axioms reduce multiplication to repeated addition.

Q6   Multiplying by 0 yields 0.

Q7 $x \times (y + 1) = (x \times y) + x$

6.10 PROBLEMS

1. By the tree test, show that arguments from one or more of the axioms of Robinson arithmetic to the following sentences are valid:
   (a) $0 \neq sss0$
   (b) $ss0 \neq sssss0$
   (c) $0 + s0 = s0$
   (d) $0 \times s0 = 0$

2. *Incompleteness of Robinson arithmetic.* The system Q is strong on particulars but weak on generalities. This, although all the particular statements:
   (a) $0 \neq s0, s0 \neq ss0, ss0 \neq sss0, \ldots$
   are provable in Q, the corresponding generalization:
   (b) $\forall x\ x \neq sx$
   is not. Similarly, none of the following generalizations are deducible from Q1 through Q7, even though all their particular instances are:
   (c) $\forall x\ (0 + x) = x$
   (d) $\forall x\ \forall y\ \forall z\ [x + (y + z)] = [(x + y) + z]$
   (e) $\forall x\ \forall y\ (x + y) = (y + x)$
   (f) $\forall x\ (0 \times x) = 0$
   (g) $\forall x\ \forall y\ (sx \times y) = [(x \times y) + y]$
   (h) $\forall x\ \forall y\ (x \times y) = (y \times x)$
   Use the tree test on the arguments from Q1 and Q2 to the first two sentences in *a*. Then prove that none of *b* through *h* follow from Q1 through Q7 by verifying that in the following interpretation Q1 through Q7 are all true but *b* through *h* are all false.

   Domain: the natural numbers together with two more distinct items *i* and *j*.

   Extension of "*s*": the usual function $1+$, with these values for the additional arguments *i* and *j*:

$$1 + i = i,\ 1 + j = j.$$

Extensions of " + " and " × ": the usual functions, with values for the additional arguments as follows, where n is a natural number, m is i or j or a natural number, k is either i or j, and $i' = j, j' = i$:

$$k + n = k, m + k = k', n \times k = k, k \times 0 = 0, k \times m = k' \text{ if } m \neq 0$$

3. *Mathematical induction.* This is a special rule of inference, reliable in interpretations having the set N of natural numbers as domain and assigning "s" the usual extension $1+$, but unreliable in others, e.g., that of problem 2 above. As usually formulated, the rule says that any property possessed by 0 and by the successors of all numbers that possess it is possessed by all natural numbers. The corresponding tree rule ("MI") puts this idea negatively: if 0 has a certain property that not all natural numbers have (e.g., the property of being less than 100), then there must be a couple of successive natural numbers (99 and 100, in this example) the first of which has the property and the second lacks it. Here is the tree rule MI, where "a" and "b" may be any names in the notation of Q so long as the second name is new to the path.*

$$
\begin{array}{c}
\ldots 0 \ldots \\
\hline
\neg \ldots a \ldots \\
\hline
\ldots b \ldots \\
\neg \ldots sb \ldots
\end{array}
$$

Note that the work of the two-line conclusion with the requirement that "b" be new would be done as well by the one-line conclusion "$\exists x (\ldots x \ldots \wedge \neg \ldots sx \ldots)$."

The rule MI can be used to construct closed trees for the arguments from Q1 through Q7 to each of b through h in problem 1. Construct such trees for the following:

(*a*) The argument "Q1, Q2, so b" in problem 2.

(*b*) The following argument form ("mathematical induction"):

$$P0, \forall x \, (Px \rightarrow Psx), \text{ so } \forall x \, Px$$

---

* The rule MI is adapted from Sue Toledo, *Tableau Systems*, Springer-Verlag, New York, 1975, p. 37 ("Complete Induction").

7

UNCOMPUTABILITY

We now turn attention from the scope of formal logic to its limits. We know that the tree test for validity of arguments of all forms found in Chapters 2 through 6 is sound and complete. But in Chapter 9 we shall prove Gödel's incompleteness theorem: neither the tree test nor any other sound general test for validity of a more powerful sort of ("second-order") arguments can be complete. That proof will use another remarkable fact, the Church-Turing theorem, proved in Chapter 8: the decision problem for first-order logic is absolutely unsolvable, i.e., in failing to provide a general decision procedure for validity of arguments of the sort found in Chapters 4 through 6 the tree test is typical of all routine procedures. (This presentation reverses the historical order; the Church and Turing proofs were inspired by Gödel's theorem, and were published five years after Gödel's proof.)

It was Turing who invented the modern stored-program digital computer. Here we are not concerned with his design of an actual electronic digital computer built in the late 1930s, but with his discovery of the very idea behind the computers that are today as plentiful as typewriters. His reason for enunciating that idea was to prove that no such device can solve the decision problem. This he proved by showing that if the decision problem were solvable, so would be a certain problem concerning computer programs—the "halting problem," which he formulated and proved unsolvable. We shall depart from his proof mainly in using as our paradigm computing machine something much like today's familiar computers, instead of the imaginary tape processing machines in terms of which Turing found it expedient to present his ideas in 1936.

7.1 HOW TO PROGRAM A REGISTER MACHINE

As the name indicates, a register machine consists of a finite number of registers—boxes, as they might be, each capable of holding any finite number of stones, so that the number stored in a register at a particular time would simply be the number of stones in that box at that time.

With that sort of hardware, a register machine program would be a set of instructions for putting single stones into registers and removing single stones from registers, i.e., adding and subtracting 1. Registers are designated by letters "A," "B," etc. Among the simplest programs (Figure 7.1a) is one that simply adds a stone to the pile in a box—in register A, say. The letter in the circle ("in the node") identifies the register to be operated upon, and the plus sign on the exit arrow identifies the operation: add 1.

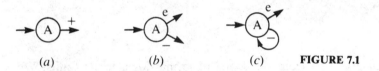

(a)   (b)   (c)   **FIGURE 7.1**

Slightly more complicated is the program that subtracts 1 from the number in a register *if possible*: see Figure 7.1b. If register A is empty, subtraction is not possible, and we leave the node on the arrow labeled "e" (for "empty"), but if there are any stones in register A, we remove one and leave on the " − " arrow.

Bending the " − " arrow back to the node as in Figure 7.1c, we have a program for emptying register A, setting the number in it equal to 0. If the register is already empty, we go straight out on the "e" arrow without doing anything. But if register A has any stones in it, we remove one and return on the " − " arrow to look once again and see whether it's now empty. If so, we go straight out on the "e" arrow; if not, we repeat the process—as many times as necessary to empty the register.

Section 7.1 was adapted from Joachim Lambek, "How to Program an Infinite Abacus," *Canadian Mathematical Bulletin*, **4**: 295–302, 1961, modifying a proposal of Z. A. Melzak's, "An Informal Arithmetical Approach to Computability and Computation," *Canadian Mathematical Bulletin*, **4**: 279–294, 1961.

Every program has a "start" arrow, coming from nowhere (from no node). Programs that don't run forever have one or more "halt" arrows, going nowhere. And some programs that do run forever have halt arrows.

The two sorts of operations illustrated above—add 1, subtract 1 unless empty—are the only ones used in register machine computations. Thus, the program of Figure 7.2a adds the number in register B to the number in register A, emptying register B in the process, and leaving the sum in register A. In detail: we remove a stone from register B and then add a stone to register A, repeating the process until register B is empty. The effect is the same as if we had simply emptied box B into box A all at once. The point illustrated by Figure 7.2a is that the same effect can be had without resorting to any operations beyond the basic two: add 1, subtract 1 unless empty.

The more complicated program of Figure 7.2b lets us add the number in register B to the number in register A without emptying B. The upper subprogram empties B into A while duplicating the original contents of B in C. Upon leaving that subprogram on the "e" arrow from the "B" node, we enter another subprogram, emptying C into B so as to restore the latter's original contents—*provided register C was empty at the beginning.* When the whole program halts, the number in register A will be the sum of the numbers originally in registers A and B.

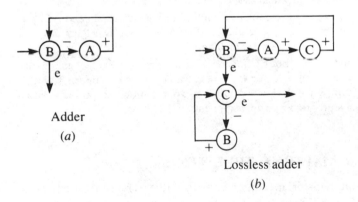

Adder

(a)

Lossless adder

(b)

FIGURE 7.2

The adder of Figure 7.2b is easily adapted to get the multiplier of Figure 7.3, where the numbers to be multiplied are in registers A and B, and registers C and D are empty initially. First, register A is emptied into D, which is then used as a counter: the number in B is added to the number in A as many times as there are stones in D, one of which is removed before each addition. When D is finally empty the number in A will be the product of the numbers initially in A and B—if C and D were initially empty.

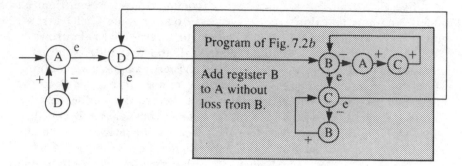

FIGURE 7.3
Multiplier.

7.2 PROBLEMS

1. Initially there are x stones in register A, y in register B, none in registers C or D. How long does it take to carry out the full program of Figure 7.3 if each passage over an arrow and through a node takes 1 second in all?

2. Initially registers A and B contain x and y stones, respectively, with all other registers empty. Program the machine to leave $x - y$ stones in register A unless that's a negative number, in which case it's to leave 0 stones there.

3. Exponentiation is repeated cumulative multiplication: y^0 is 1 and y^{x+1} is $y^x \times y$—so that for positive x, y^x is the product of xy's. Using Figure 7.3 as a "black box," design a program for exponentiation.

4. (Solved at the end of the book.) Superexponentiation is repeated cumulative exponentiation: $\sup(x, 0) = 1$, $\sup(x, 1) = x$, $\sup(x, 2) = x^x$, $\sup(x, 3) = x^{(x^x)}$, and in general, $\sup(x, y + 1) = x^{\sup(x, y)}$. Using your solution to problem 3 as a black box, design a program for superexponentiation.

7.3 REGISTER MACHINE TREE TESTS

We have seen that register machines can do rather elaborate numerical computations. We shall now see how they can also do elaborate non-numerical computations—in particular, tree tests. It's a matter of coding sentences and finite sets of sentences and truth trees as single numbers, called "Gödel numbers" after Kurt Gödel, who used the coding trick in proving his famous incompleteness theorem (Chapter 9). The thing can be done in various ways. We'll do it by reading the symbols out of which trees are built as digits in the base N system of notation, N being the number of distinct symbols used in representing trees. Let's see how that might go when the notation is that of "RA" (as we'll call it), i.e., Robinson arithmetic (Section 6.9) augmented by a symbol "\" for exponentiation.

The symbols in the upper row of the following display will be treated as digits in the base $N = 18$ system of notation, with the numerical values shown in the lower row:

)	(	∀	∃	x	y	→	¬	0	s	=	+	×	\	′	#	✓	|
0	1	2	3	4	5	6	7	8	9	10	11	12	13	14	15	16	17

In this odd notation, the digit for zero is the right-hand parenthesis.* The base 18 digits for 1 through 12 are other symbols of Robinson arithmetic. The base 18 digit for 13 will be used for the exponential function: we shall write x^y on a single line as "$x\backslash y$," and add Q8 and Q9 below as new axioms of RA:

Q8 $\forall x\, (x\backslash 0) = s0$ (since $x^0 = 1$)

Q9 $\forall x\, \forall y\, (x\backslash sy) = (x\backslash y) \times x$ (since $x^{y+1} = x^y \times x$)

The accent (base 18 digit for 14) will be used when the variables x and y aren't enough, to get further variables x', y', x'', etc. Since " $\times$ " is used for multiplication in Robinson arithmetic, we use " # " (base 18 digit for 15) to close paths in trees. Finally, the vertical bar (base 18 digit for 17) is used to separate lists.

Now the axioms and theorems of RA are base 18 number names, e.g., axiom Q8 is a base 18 name of this number.

$$2{\cdot}18^9 + 4{\cdot}18^8 + 1{\cdot}18^7 + 4{\cdot}18^6 + 13{\cdot}18^5 + 8{\cdot}18^4 + 0{\cdot}18^3$$
$$+ 10{\cdot}18^2 + 9{\cdot}18^1 + 8{\cdot}18^0$$

Truth trees can also be read as base 18 number names. Thus, a tree like:

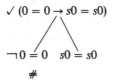

is viewed as a pair of paths:

$$\checkmark\, (0 = 0 \to s0 = s0) \qquad \checkmark\, (0 = 0 \to s0 = s0)$$
$$\neg\, 0 = 0 \qquad\qquad s0 = s0$$
$$\#$$

---

* Chosen because it's never the beginning of a sentence. If different sentences are to have different code numbers, zero had better not be a possible first digit.

Each is written horizontally, using bars as punctuation:

$| \checkmark \ (0 = 0 \rightarrow s0 = s0)| \neg 0 = 0 | \# |$ $| \checkmark \ (0 = 0 \rightarrow s0 = s0)| s0 = s0 |$

When we run them together to get a base 18 number name, we get:

$| \checkmark \ (0 = 0 \rightarrow s0 = s0)| \neg 0 = 0 | \# \| \checkmark \ (0 = 0 \rightarrow s0 = s0)| s0 = s0 |$

in which the double bar marks the separation between the two lists.

Thus symbols, sentences, and truth trees stand for numbers in the base 18 system of notation; base 18 number names are texts. It's texts that we manipulate in carrying out the tree program, number names that we manipulate in carrying out numerical computations; but where the texts are sentences of Robinson arithmetic or trees of such sentences, texts *are* number names in our base 18 system of notation.

If we think of registers as boxes and of the machine language as using the base 1 system, with the number in a register being the number of stones in the box, we need an input–output routine to translate base 18 texts into base 1 piles of stones and vice versa, in order to use register machines as text processors. That's straightforward. Alternatively, we could use machines whose hardware is adapted to our base 18 notation, just as commercially available machines use hardware adapted to the base 2 notation and as old desk calculators used hardware adapted to the base 10 notation. The basic operations of adding and subtracting 1 would not be matters of moving single stones, but those operations could be engineered straightforwardly. Such machines would be user-friendly for text processing, but relatively awkward for numerical calculation.

Take your choice; register machine programs don't know what sort of hardware they're being run on. Any operation on a text, e.g., application of UI to "$\forall x \neg 0 = sx$" in order to get "$\neg 0 = s0$," can be accomplished step by step by appropriately chosen small changes of the $+1$ and -1 sort in base 18 notation.*

Here are some exercises in base 18 arithmetic:

1. What sentence of Robinson arithmetic has the smallest Gödel number?
2. What text has 1 + the answer to problem 1 as its Gödel number?
3. In base 18 notation (a) add $s)))$ to $0 = 0$, (b) add $0\forall |)$ to $0 = 0$, (c) subtract $0 = 0$ from $0 = s0$.

---

* For example, since in base 18 "0" means 8 and "x" means 4, four applications of $+1$ transform $\forall x \neg 0 = sx$ into $\forall x \neg 0 = s0$. Then $2 \cdot 18^6 + 4 \cdot 18^5$ applications of -1 change that into $\neg 0 = s0$.

7.4   THE CHURCH-TURING THESIS

> Register machines can be programmed to compute any functions that
> are computable at all.

For all their simplicity, register machines are capable of remarkable computational feats. We have seen how such familiar functions as addition, multiplication, and exponentiation can be computed by register machines and—in general terms—how text-processing programs like the tree test can be run on register machines. Further experience with programming these machines shows them capable of computing a very wide range of other functions, familiar and unfamiliar, simple and complex. Although register machine programs represent only a very special sort of clerical routine for computing functions whose arguments and values are natural numbers, it appears that every other sort of clerical routine can be transcribed for the register machine. Thus routines written in various programming languages and carried out on various commercially available electronic computers can be rewritten in the form illustrated above and carried out on register machines, to the same effect.

The Church-Turing thesis is the hypothesis that indeed no clerical routine that ever has been or can be invented is more powerful than the routines we have been examining, that register machines can perform; it is the hypothesis that if a function is computable at all, it is computable by some register machine program. This thesis is not susceptible of mathematical proof, for there is no limit to the variety of forms that clerical routines might assume, and thus no general, precise definition of the term "clerical routine" of the sort we would need in order to prove the Church-Turing thesis. In contrast, the notion of register machine program is very clear and can be defined quite precisely. The same is true of every other particular sort of clerical routine, but the general notion of clerical routine defies precise definition.

Although the Church-Turing thesis cannot be proved, it might be refuted, if false. For if it is false there will be some particular, precisely specifiable clerical routine that allows one to compute some definite function f that no register machine program can compute. Since the general term "register machine program" is precisely definable, we can hope to prove that no such program computes f.

Thus, the Church-Turing thesis is refutable if false, but stands so far unrefuted. Confidence in it is based on the fact that perverse human ingenuity has not managed to invent a clerical routine that can't be transcribed for the register machine.

7.5 UNSOLVABILITY OF THE HALTING PROBLEM

We now define a certain function h, and prove that no register machine program computes it. According to the Church-Turing thesis that means that the function h is absolutely uncomputable.

The definition of h refers to an enumeration $f_0, f_1, f_2, \ldots$ of all functions of one variable that are computable by register machine programs. We can think of that enumeration as derived from a prior enumeration P_0, $P_1, P_2, \ldots$ of all register machine programs. For definiteness, we suppose that the distinct registers used in the computation are designated "A," "B," "C," "D," "A′," "B′," etc., in order. To derive the enumeration of functions from the enumeration of programs, think of the argument n as initially stored in register A, and of the value $f_m(n)$ as stored in register A when the program halts. Now to compute $f_m(n)$, identify the program P_m and set it to work with n stones in register A and all other registers empty. If the program ever halts, the value $f_m(n)$ will be the number in register A at that time; and if the program never halts, $f_m(n)$ is understood to be undefined.

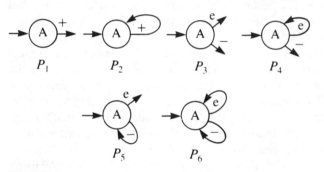

FIGURE 7.4
The six 1-node programs.

Details of the enumeration of programs are unimportant so long as it is a routine matter to determine what program P_m is, for each $m = 0, 1, 2, \ldots$, and so long as all register machine programs appear in the list. But it's natural to take P_0 to be the 0-node program, the graph of which is simply an arrow. That program halts immediately, regardless of what may be in any of the machine's registers. (The fact that there are no nodes in the program's graph doesn't mean that the machine it's "run" on has no registers.) This program leaves the contents of register A unchanged; it computes the identity function:

$$f_0(n) = n$$

Next we might take the six 1-node programs (Figure 7.4) that compute the following functions:

$$f_1(n) = n + 1 \qquad\qquad f_4(n) = \begin{cases} \text{undefined} & \text{if } n = 0 \\ n - 1 & \text{if } n \neq 0 \end{cases}$$

$$f_2(n) = \text{undefined for all } n \qquad f_5(n) = 0$$

$$f_3(n) = \begin{cases} 0 & \text{if } n = 0 \\ n - 1 & \text{if } n \neq 0 \end{cases} \qquad f_6(n) = \text{undefined for all } n$$

And the list might continue with the 2-node programs, the 3-node programs, etc. To specify the enumeration exactly one would have to determine an order for the programs within each of these blocks, but as the thing can be done in various ways, which are equally good for our purposes, we shall not trouble to fix details.

Once an enumeration of programs is fixed, a function h can be defined:

$$h(n) = \begin{cases} 0 & \text{if } f_n(n) \text{ is undefined} \\ 1 & \text{if } f_n(n) \text{ is defined} \end{cases}$$

The letter "h" is for "halt": $h(n)$ is 1 or 0 depending on whether or not program P_n eventually halts, once started with its own serial number n in register A and all other registers empty.

The **self-halting** problem is the problem of devising a register machine program that computes the function h.

Is there such a program? If so, we can easily modify it so as to get a program that computes the function g defined as follows:

$$g(n) = \begin{cases} 0 & \text{if } f_n(n) \text{ is undefined} \\ \text{undefined} & \text{if } f_n(n) \text{ is defined} \end{cases}$$

The method is shown in Figure 7.5, which is drawn for the case in which the h program has exactly two *halt* arrows. (The actual number doesn't matter, but there will surely be at least one.) In Figure 7.5 these are *start*

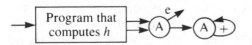

FIGURE 7.5
Converting a program that computes h into one that computes g.

arrows for an additional two-node program that halts or goes on forever depending on whether the h program left 0 or 1 in register A. Clearly the program of Figure 7.5 exists if the h program does—and computes the function g.

Suppose, then, that some program computes g—whether or not of the particular shape indicated in Figure 7.5. If there is one, it will appear somewhere in our exhaustive list of register machine programs—say, in the mth place, as program P_m. Then for each n, $f_m(n) = g(n)$ if either side of the equation is defined, and each side will be undefined if the other is. Therefore we can replace the left-hand side of our definition of g, above, by "f_m." Doing so, and then setting $n = m$, we deduce this:

$$f_m(m) = \begin{cases} 0 & \text{if } f_m(m) \text{ is undefined} \\ \text{undefined} & \text{if } f_m(m) \text{ is defined} \end{cases}$$

But that's self-contradictory: it says that if $f_m(m)$ is undefined if it's defined, and defined if it's undefined.

It follows that the function g is computable by no register machine program. But this means that h isn't computable by any register machine program either, for Figure 7.5 shows how to turn an h computer into a g computer; if there can be no g computer, there can be no h computer either. We have found that the self-halting problem for register machine programs is not solvable by register machine programs.

It also follows that the *halting* problem for register machine programs is unsolvable by such programs. That's the problem of deciding for arbitrary natural numbers m and n whether or not P_m eventually halts, if started with n stones in register A and all others empty—the problem of deciding whether or not $f_m(n)$ is defined. The self-halting problem is reducible to the halting problem in the sense that a solution to the latter would solve the former as well: just set $m = n$ and use the solution to the halting problem to discover whether or not $f_n(n)$ is defined. Since the self-halting problem is unsolvable, so is the halting problem.

If the Church-Turing thesis is true, this shows that the halting problem for register machine programs is *absolutely* unsolvable: solvable by no routine of any sort.

Warning: Unsolvability of the self-halting problem does not mean that there are non-self-halters that cannot be recognized as such or proved to be such. For there's always a fact of the matter—whether or not $f_n(n)$ is defined, for a particular natural number n—and in the case of any particular non-self-halter, we may be lucky or ingenious enough to recognize and prove that it never halts. Unsolvability of the problem means only that there is no general mechanical routine for recognizing non-self-halters.

7.6 PROBLEMS

These are solved at the back of the book.

1. *The busy beaver.* Define $r(n)$ as the running time of the longest-running n-node register machine programs that eventually halt when started with all registers empty. Here *running time = number of passages through nodes*, e.g., $r(0) = 0,$* $r(1) = 1$, and $r(2) = 3.$†

   (*a*) What is the running time of the program shown in Figure 7.6*a*? Bearing in mind that this may not be the longest-running $(n + 1)$ node program, what follows about $r(n + 1)$?

   (*b*) See Figure 7.6*b*. Show that $m > n$ if $r(m) > r(n)$.

   (*c*) See Figure 7.6*c*. Show that if r is computable (say, by a k-node program R that doesn't use register B), then $r(n + k + 2) \geq r[r(n)].$‡

   (*d*) Prove unsolvable the "busy beaver" problem of designing a register machine program that computes $r.$¶

2. *Unsolvability of the self-halting problem.* Use the Church-Turing thesis to reduce the busy beaver problem to the halting problem for register machine programs; i.e., explain in general terms how to turn a solution of the halting problem into a solution of the busy beaver problem.

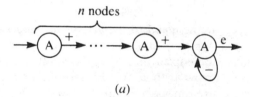

(*a*)

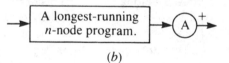

(*b*)

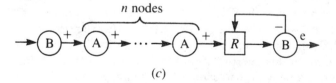

(*c*)

FIGURE 7.6

---

* In Figure 7.4 the empty start running time of P_n is 1 for $n = 0, 2, 4$ and 0 for $n = 1, 3, 5$.

† Figure 7.6*a* is one of the longest-running 2-node programs starting with all registers empty.

‡ *Hint:* How many passages through nodes does it take to put n stones into a register?

¶ *Hint:* Show that if the problem were solvable, k would be bigger than any natural number. This problem (and its solution) is adapted from Tibor Rado, "On Computable Functions," *Bell System Technical Journal*, **41**: 877–884, 1962.

7.7   PROGRAMS IN LOGICAL NOTATION

The informal, vivid graphical representation that we have been using for register machine programs is one of many possibilities. Our purposes in Chapters 8 and 9 are better served by using sets of sentences in logical notation to represent programs P_m that compute functions of one variable.* These sentences don't use the sign " = " of identity, and do use three special symbols: a name "0," a one-place function symbol "s," and a predicate letter "R" that has two more places than the number of distinct registers referred to in the program's description. In the intended interpretation, the domain is the set of all natural numbers, the extension of "0" is the number zero, the extension of "s" is the successor function $1+$, and the extension of "R" is a set of sequences of natural numbers determined by the program P_m and the initial contents of the machine's registers, as follows.

> The sequence $(t, p, q, r, \ldots)$ is in the extension of "R" iff at time t, carrying out the program, we are traversing arrow p, with q stones in register A, r in register B, etc.

Natural numbers $q = 0, 1, 2, \ldots$ are assigned to the arrows in the graph of P_m sequentially, starting with 0 for the "start" arrow. We suppose that when the program runs, it takes some fixed time (say, 1 second) to traverse a node, going from the entering arrow at time t to the appropriate existing arrow at time $t + 1$. These successive times are numbered $t = 0, 1, 2, \ldots$.

It follows that $(t, p, q, r, \ldots)$ doesn't belong to the extension of "R" if the program halts before time t, or if p isn't one of the numbers assigned to arrows. Otherwise, $(t, p, q, r, \ldots)$ *may* belong to the extension of "R"; whether it actually does depends on the number initially in register A and on the program.

An example is provided by the flowchart of Figure 7.7. Since there are four arrows, they are numbered 0, 1, 2, 3. Since two distinct registers are named in the nodes, "R" is a four-place predicate letter. Its extension is the set $\{(0, 0, 2, 0), (1, 3, 2, 0)\}$, for as register B is initially empty, it is arrows 0 and 3 that are traversed. In this interpretation the sentences "$R00ss00$" and "$RsOsssOssOO$" are true and all other sentences beginning with "R" are false.†

In this notation we can describe the graph of Figure 7.7, using a universally quantified conditional for each pair of arrows that respectively enter and exit the same node. The antecedent of the conditional corre-

---

* The following representation was devised by George Boolos in 1974.
† That is, beginning with "R" when no parentheses are omitted. Thus, "$R0000 \rightarrow R0000$" is true but begins with "(," not "R," being short for "$(R0000 \rightarrow R0000)$."

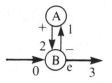

Initially there are two
stones in register A,
none in register B.   **FIGURE 7.7**

sponds to the arrow entering the node, the consequent to the arrow exiting it. Certain details will be determined by what's written in the node and by the label on the exiting arrow. In Figure 7.7 there are five such pairs. These are shown in Figure 7.8 together with the corresponding quantified conditionals. Only the second of these represents a path traversed when the program is run with two stones in register A and none in register B initially, but we write out the statements corresponding to all pairs in order to describe the program itself, apart from register contents.

$\xrightarrow{0}$ (B) $\xrightarrow[-]{1}$	$(0, 1-)$	$\forall x\ \forall y\ \forall z\ (Rx0ysz \rightarrow Rsxs0yz)$
$\xrightarrow{0}$ (B) $\xrightarrow[e]{3}$	$(0, 3e)$	$\forall x\ \forall y\ (Rx0y0 \rightarrow Rsxsss0y0)$
$\xrightarrow{1}$ (A) $\xrightarrow[+]{2}$	$(1, 2+)$	$\forall x\ \forall y\ \forall z\ (Rxs0yz \rightarrow Rsxss0syz)$
$\xrightarrow{2}$ (B) $\xrightarrow[-]{1}$	$(2, 1-)$	$\forall x\ \forall y\ \forall z\ (Rxss0ysz \rightarrow Rsxs0yz)$
$\xrightarrow{2}$ (B) $\xrightarrow[e]{3}$	$(2, 3e)$	$\forall x\ \forall y\ (Rxss0y0 \rightarrow Rsxsss0y0)$

FIGURE 7.8
Transition sentences for Figure 7.7.

There are three kinds of sentences in Figure 7.8, one for each of the three possible labels on exit arrows. The number of the entry arrow i and the number and type of the exit arrow j are indicated in parentheses at the left of each transition sentence. The general scheme is the following, where the transition sentences are abbreviated, and "v" represents the variable for the number of stones in the register named in the node.

Type	Abbreviated Transition Sentence
$(i, j+)$	$R(x, i, \ldots, v, \ldots) \rightarrow R(x + 1, j, \ldots, v + 1, \ldots)$
$(i, j-)$	$R(x, i, \ldots, v + 1, \ldots) \rightarrow R(x + 1, j, \ldots, v, \ldots)$
(i, je)	$R(x, i, \ldots, 0, \ldots) \rightarrow R(x + 1, j, \ldots, 0, \ldots)$

In this abbreviated notation the five sentences in Fig. 7.8 would be written as follows, omitting quantifiers to reduce clutter and decoding "sx" as

"$x + 1$," "$s0$" as "1," etc., so that "$RsxssOsyz$" becomes "$R(x + 1, 2, y + 1, z)$," etc.

$(0, 1-)$	$R(x, 0, y, z + 1) \rightarrow R(x + 1, 1, y, z)$
$(0, 3e)$	$R(x, 0, y, 0) \rightarrow R(x + 1, 3, y, 0)$
$(1, 2+)$	$R(x, 1, y, z) \rightarrow R(x + 1, 2, y + 1, z)$
$(2, 1-)$	$R(x, 2, y, z + 1) \rightarrow R(x + 1, 1, y, z)$
$(2, 3e)$	$R(x, 2, y, 0) \rightarrow R(x + 1, 3, y, 0)$

Restoring these to the unabbreviated notation of Figure 7.8 is a matter of dropping commas and parentheses, recoding "$x + 1$" as "sx," "1" as "$s0$," etc., enclosing each conditional in parentheses, and then universally quantifying all of its variables at the far left.

7.8 PROBLEMS

Describe programs 1 to 3 of Figure 7.9 in the full notation of Figure 7.8 and the abbreviated notation just illustrated. Indicate the type of each transition.

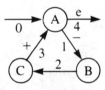

Empty register A
while copying it
into B and C.

(1)

Empty register A.

(This needs four
quantified
conditionals.)

(2)

Fill register A
endlessly.

(3)

FIGURE 7.9

UNDECIDABILITY

We have seen that the tree test for validity or consistency needn't always terminate, e.g., the tests for validity of the argument "$\forall x \, \exists y \, Lxy$, so Laa" and consistency of the sentence "$\forall x \, Lxfx$" produce trees that grow forever:

1	$\forall x \, \exists y \, Lxy$	(premise)		1	$\forall x \, Lxfx$	(consistent?)
2	$\neg Laa$	($\neg$ conclusion)		2	$Lafa$	(from 1)
3	$\checkmark \exists y \, Lay$	(from 1)		3	$Lfaffa$	(from 2)
4	Lab	(from 3)		4	$Lffafffa$	(from 3)
5	$\checkmark \exists y \, Lby$	(from 1)		5	$Lfffaffffa$	(from 4)
6	Lbc	(from 5)		6	$Lffffafffffa$	(from 5)
7	$\checkmark \exists y \, Lcy$	(from 1)		7	$Lfffffaffffffa$	(from 6)
8	Lcd	(from 7)		8	$Lffffffafffffffa$	(from 7)
etc.				etc.		

These open paths determine interpretations in which the initial lists are true, on the basis of which we see that the argument tested at the left is invalid, and that the sentence tested at the right is consistent. We see that, but a machine programmed to carry out the tests according to the flow diagram of Figure 6.1 would not, for it would go forever round the loop from stages 2 through 6 and back to 2, never answering "Yes" to the question at stage 2 or "No" to the question at stage 6, never deciding about validity of the argument or consistency of the sentence.

8.1   THE DECISION PROBLEM

The obvious move is to refine the tree test so that the program can determine that the tree it's generating will grow forever, halting at that point with the decision that the argument is invalid or that the set is consistent. That needn't be an easy task, for infinite trees need not be like our two examples, slim and orderly. All the more glory, then, to the discoverer of a decision procedure for validity and consistency.

But the task is worse than difficult; it is impossible. There can be no formal decision procedure for validity or consistency. In this respect the tree test is typical of all computational procedures, for the decision problem is unsolvable. In 1936 that was proved twice: by Alonzo Church in Princeton, New Jersey, and—independently and slightly later—by Alan Turing in Cambridge, England. Here we give a version of Turing's proof, showing that any register machine program that solved the decision problem for validity of arguments could be used to compute the function h that was seen in Section 7.5 to be uncomputable by register machine programs.* That will prove the following:

Church-Turing theorem. Unsolvable by register machine programs: the decision problem for validity and consistency.

Then if the Church-Turing thesis is true, the decision problem is absolutely unsolvable.

The proof goes like this. With any natural number n and register machine program P_m described in the logical notation of Section 7.7, we associate an argument (Section 8.2) that's valid or invalid depending on whether or not P_m eventually halts if started with n stones in register A and all other registers empty (Section 8.3). Thus a test that solved the decision problem, correctly classifying all arguments as valid or not, would thereby solve the halting problem that was proved unsolvable in Section 7.5. Conclusion: the decision problem is unsolvable.

Any adequate test (e.g., the tree test) will classify the argument as valid if (completeness) and only if (soundness) it really is valid. So, since the tree method for recognizing *valid* arguments and *inconsistent* sets of sentences

---

* The present proof (devised by George Boolos in 1974) is a considerable simplification of Turing's original proof (1936–1937).

could be programmed for a register machine, the existence of register machine programs that recognize invalid arguments and consistent sets of sentences would solve the decision problem. Then when we have proved the Church-Turing theorem, we shall have proved the following as well:

Corollary. Unsolvable by register machine programs: the general problem of recognizing *invalidity* of arguments with finite numbers of premises and *consistency* of finite sets of sentences.

8.2 A ROUTINE TEST FOR HALTING

Given the number n of stones initially in register A (all other registers being empty) and a set of sentences representing a program P_m in the notation of Section 7.7, it is straightforward to write out an argument in that notation (the "associated argument") that's valid iff the program eventually halts (Section 8.3).

Example 1. The program of Figure 7.7 starts with two stones in register A ($n = 2$) and none in B. Here, the first premise

$$(\text{Init}) \quad R00ss00$$

describes the initial configuration, the remaining five premises are the transition sentences of Figure 7.7, and the conclusion

$$(\text{Halt}) \quad \exists x\, \exists y\, \exists z\, Rxsss0yz$$

says that at some time (x) the halt arrow (3) is traversed, i.e., the program eventually halts.

Example 2. Program 1 of Figure 7.8 starts with n stones initially in register A and the other registers initially empty. As there are three registers, the predicate letter "R" has 5 places.

(Init)	$R00sss\ldots000$ (n symbols "s")
$(0, 1-)$	$\forall x\, \forall y\, \forall z\, \forall w\, (Rx0syzw \to Rsxs0yzw)$
$(0, 4e)$	$\forall x\, \forall z\, \forall w\, (Rx00zw \to Rsxsss0zw)$
$(1, 2+)$	$\forall x\, \forall y\, \forall z\, \forall w\, (Rxs0yzw \to Rsxss0yszw)$
$(2, 3+)$	$\forall x\, \forall y\, \forall z\, \forall w\, (Rxss0yzw \to Rsxsss0yzsw)$
$(3, 1-)$	$\forall x\, \forall y\, \forall z\, \forall w\, (Rx0sss0syzw \to Rsxs0yzw)$
$(3, 4e)$	$\forall x\, \forall z\, \forall w\, (Rxsss00zw \to Rsxssss0zw)$
(Halt)	$\exists x\, \exists y\, \exists z\, \exists w\, Rxssss0yzw$

Here it is again, in summary notation, as a set of sentences that's inconsistent iff the corresponding inference is valid, with the denial of the conclusion rewritten as "$\forall x\, \forall y\, \forall z\, \forall w\, \neg\, Rxsssss0yzw$" so that in each line all absent quantifiers can be taken as universal.

(Init)	$R(0, 0, n, 0, 0)$
(0, 1$-$)	$R(x, 0, y + 1, z, w) \rightarrow R(x + 1, 1, y, z, w)$
(0, 4e)	$R(x, 0, 0, z, w) \rightarrow R(x + 1, 4, 0, z, w)$
(1, 2$+$)	$R(x, 1, y, z, w) \rightarrow R(x + 1, 2, y, z + 1, w)$
(2, 3$+$)	$R(x, 2, y, z, w) \rightarrow R(x + 1, 3, y, z, w + 1)$
(3, 1$-$)	$R(x, 3, y + 1, z, w) \rightarrow R(x + 1, 1, y, z, w)$
(3, 4e)	$R(x, 3, 0, z, w) \rightarrow R(x + 1, 4, 0, z, w)$
($\neg$ Halt)	$\neg R(x, 4, y, z, w)$

Example 3—no exit. Where there is no exit arrow, as Fig. 7.9(3), the program cannot halt. Any sentence not implied by the premises will serve as conclusion. The simplest such sentence expressible in our notation is the denial

$$\text{(Halt)} \quad \neg\, R00\dots$$

of the first premise (init). We can depend on this argument to be invalid because we can depend on its premises to form a consistent set, being true in the intended interpretation.*

Example 4—more than one exit. Where there are two or more exit arrows—say, three, numbered 5, 18, and 19—the conclusion will be an existentially quantified statement saying that one or another halt arrow is traversed

$$\text{(Halt)} \quad \exists x \dots [R(x, 5, \dots) \lor R(x, 18, \dots) \lor R(x, 19, \dots)]$$

8.3 THE ARGUMENT IS VALID IFF THE PROGRAM HALTS

It is time to prove the claim made in Section 8.2 for the argument associated with a program P_m and a number n: The argument is valid iff the program would eventually halt, once started with n stones in register A and all other registers empty. Otherwise put: the associated argument is valid iff $f_m(n)$ is defined.

---

* As the denial of the conclusion is logically equivalent to the first premise, the set consisting of the premises with the denial of the conclusion is consistent iff the set consisting of just the premises is.

In the "only if" direction, the proof is trivial, for by design all premises of the associated argument are true (in the interpretation specified in Section 7.7) and its conclusion was designed to be true (in that interpretation) iff $f_m(n)$ is defined. Then if the argument is valid, its conclusion is true (in that interpretation) and $f_m(n)$ is defined. Thus the argument is valid only if $f_m(n)$ is defined.

In the rest of this chapter we'll simply use "true" instead of "true in the interpretation specified in Section 7.7."

In the "if" direction the proof is easy but not trivial. We first prove a lemma:

> If the program hasn't halted by then, a description of time t is deducible from the premises of the associated argument.

"Descriptions of time t" are sentences of form

$$R(t, p, q, r, \ldots)$$

—i.e., the corresponding sentences in unabbreviated notation. Any such description is true if deducible from the premises of the associated argument, all of which are true.

Note that (1) there are no true descriptions of time t if the program has halted by then and (2), otherwise, there is one and only one true description of time t.

We prove the lemma by mathematical induction. Such proofs have two stages: a "basis," in which the thing is proved in the special case of $t = 0$, and an "induction step," in which we prove (for all t) that if the thing is true for one value of t, then it's true for the next as well, i.e., for $t + 1$.

For the basis, since the first premise of the associated argument is a description of time 0, such a description is deducible.

The lemma is the universal quantification of a conditional of form "$\neg H(t) \to D(t)$," where "$H(t)$" means that the program has halted by time t and "$D(t)$" means that a description of time t is deducible from the premises of the associated argument. Then for the induction step we need to prove that for all natural numbers t

$$[\neg H(t) \to D(t)] \to [\neg H(t + 1) \to D(t + 1)] \tag{1}$$

It is an exercise in truth-functional logic to verify that formula 1 follows from

$$[D(t) \wedge \neg H(t + 1)] \to D(t + 1) \tag{2}$$

together with the obvious truth

$$H(t) \to H(t + 1) \tag{3}$$

that if the program has halted by time t, then it has halted by time $t + 1$.

Then for the induction step it suffices to prove formula 2, i.e., in English:

> If a description of time t follows from the premises of the associated argument and the program hasn't halted by time $t + 1$, then a description of time $t + 1$ also follows.

There are three possibilities to be considered, depending on which of the three types of transitions took us from time t, traversing arrow i, to time $t + 1$, traversing arrow j.

First type: $(1, j+)$

$$R(x, i, \ldots, v, \ldots) \to R(x + 1, j, \ldots, v + 1, \ldots)$$

The conditional at the right appears with all variables universally quantifed as a premise of the associated argument. Then by as many steps of UI as there are variables we deduce the sentence

$$R(t, i, \ldots, r, \ldots) \to R(t + 1, j, \ldots, r + 1, \ldots)$$

in which the antecedent is the description of time t that follows from the premises of the associated argument. Then the consequent also follows from them. As it's a description of time $t + 1$, the induction step is proved in this case.

Second type: $(i, j-)$

$$R(x, i, \ldots, v + 1, \ldots) \to R(x + 1, j, \ldots, v, \ldots)$$

Here again the conditional appears with all variables universally quantified as a premise of the associated argument, so that by as many steps of UI as there are variables, we deduce the sentence

$$R(t, i, \ldots, r + 1, \ldots) \to (R(t + 1, j, \ldots, r, \ldots)$$

in which the antecedent is the description of time t that follows from the premises of the associated argument. Then a description of time $t + 1$ also follows, i.e., the consequent.

Third type: (i, je)

$$R(x, i, \ldots, 0, \ldots) \to R(x + 1, j, \ldots, 0, \ldots)$$

Again the conditional appears with all variables universally quantified as a premise of the associated argument, and by as many steps of UI as there are variables, we deduce the sentence

$$R(t, i, \ldots, 0, \ldots) \to R(t + 1, j, \ldots, 0, \ldots)$$

in which the antecedent is the description of time t that follows from the premises of the associated argument. Then the consequent also follows, i.e., a description of time $t + 1$.

Now the induction step is proved for all three types of transitions. That these are all the possible types is guaranteed by the hypothesis (in the statement of the induction step) that the program doesn't halt before time $t + 1$, from which we conclude that the arrow i traversed in time t cannot be a halt arrow. If follows that it must terminate in some node, and hence that the transition must be one of our three types.

We have proved the lemma. It remains only to get from there to the "if" direction of the theorem: The associated argument is valid if the program halts.

Suppose, then, that the program halts—at time t, say, by traversing exit arrow i. Then it doesn't halt before t, and the lemma assures us that the premises of the associated argument imply a (true) description

$$R(t, i, \ldots) \tag{4}$$

of time t. It's clear that the argument from that sentence to its existential generalization, indicated as follows,

$$\exists x \ldots R(x, i, \ldots) \tag{5}$$

is valid. If the program has just one halt arrow, the conclusion of that argument is the conclusion of the associated argument. If the program has two or more halt arrows, the conclusion of the associated argument is an existentially quantified disjunction that's deducible from formula 4 because one of its disjuncts is, i.e., formula 5. In either case we can deduce the conclusion of the associated argument from the description of time t, and, so, from the premises of the associated argument. The case in which the conclusion of the associated argument is the denial of its first premise cannot arise if the program halts, for to halt it needs an exit arrow. Then if the program eventually halts, the associated argument is valid.

Thus the associated argument really is valid iff the program halts. It follows that we could parlay any solution to the decision problem for quantificational logic into what we know cannot exist—a solution of the halting problem for register machine programs. The Church-Turing theorem is proved.

8.4 FOCUSING THE UNDECIDABILITY RESULT

We have proved unsolvable the general decision problem for quantificational validity. We did that by reducing the halting problem for register machine programs to the decision problem for validity of a certain special class of arguments: we proved that if the decision problem were solvable, so would be the halting problem that we proved unsolvable in Section 7.5.

What are the salient features of this special class of arguments whose decision problem for validity we've proved unsolvable? The answer is

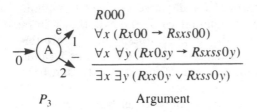

$R000$	$R000$
$\forall x\,(Rx00 \rightarrow Rsxs00)$	$\forall x\,(Rx00 \rightarrow Rsxs00)$
$\forall x\,\forall y\,(Rx0sy \rightarrow Rsxss0y)$	$\forall x\,\forall y\,(Rx0sy \rightarrow Rsxss0y)$
$\exists x\,\exists y\,(Rxs0y \lor Rxss0y)$	$\forall x\,\forall y\,\neg\,(Rxs0y \lor Rxss0y)$

P_3 Argument   Set

FIGURE 8.1
Program, associated argument, associated set.

clearly suggested by the simplest examples. In considering these it becomes clear that we do best to ask, not about the arguments themselves, but about the associated sets of sentences, whose consistency or inconsistency come to the same thing as invalidity or validity of the arguments.

Example. Validity of the associated argument for P_3 (Figure 8.1) comes to the same as inconsistency of the set whose members are the sentences in the box, where the denial of the conclusion of the argument is transformed into a logically equivalent universally quantified sentence.

As this example suggests, the set of sentences associated with a program P_m, which are inconsistent iff $f_m(n)$ is defined, has the following characteristics:

1. The set is finite.
2. Each member of the set is an "$\forall$ sentence"; i.e., any quantifiers in it form a single block at the extreme left ("prenex") and are all universal ("$\forall$").
3. The sign " = " of identity isn't used.
4. Function symbols are used (i.e. a particular one-place function symbol "s").

Then our undecidability result can be focused more narrowly.

> I. Unsolvable: the decision problem for consistency of finite sets of $\forall$ sentences without identity, in which function symbols may occur.

Note well: The claim is not that such sets can't be recognized as consistent when they are, for, e.g., it is clear that the tree test for consistency at the beginning of this chapter will never terminate, so it is clear that the set {"$\forall x\ Lxfx$"} is consistent even though it belongs to a class of sets for which the consistency decision problem is unsolvable. The claim is rather that even if consistency of sets of that sort is discoverable in each case, there is no uniform clerical routine for doing it.

8.5   A SOLVABLE CASE OF THE DECISION PROBLEM

In the absence of function symbols, the tree method provides a decision procedure for consistency of sets of ∀ sentences.

> II. Solvable: the decision problem for consistency of finite sets of ∀ sentences without function symbols—with or without identity.

Proof. As any quantifiers are universal and at the extreme left, the only names that ever appear in the tree are the finite number of them that appear initially—unless there are no names initially, in which case only one name will ever appear, i.e., the one mandated by UI in that case. Then after a finite number of applications of UI and the rules for identity, the only rules remaining to be applied will be those for the connectives, and as we saw in Section 2.8, the process of applying those rules must terminate after some finite number of steps. At that point we shall be extruded from the flowchart through one of the stop arrows, with a classification of the initial set of sentences as consistent or as inconsistent.

Evidently it's the *generic* decision problem of type I that's unsolvable, for as we've just seen, there's an important species (II) of that genus that is solvable.

In conclusion we note how using different sorts of associated arguments would have yielded two further results.

8.6   UNDECIDABILITY WITHOUT FUNCTION SYMBOLS

> III. Unsolvable: the decision problem for consistency of finite sets of sentences without function symbols—with or without identity.

We won't prove this claim, but illustrate the new sort of associated set of sentences in the case of P_3 in Figure 8.1. It will be obvious from that how the reduction would go in general. The main novelty is use of the sign of identity together with a two-place predicate symbol "S" to do the work of the function symbol "s." In the intended interpretation, the extension of "S" is the set of ordered pairs $(m, m + 1)$, where m is any natural number. Thus, "Sxy" will mean that the successor of x is y, i.e., $x + 1 = y$.

Here are the sentences in the new set associated with P_3:

1. $\forall x \, \exists y \, Sxy$ (existence of successors)
2. $\forall x \, \forall y \, \forall z \, [(Sxy \wedge Sxz) \rightarrow y = z]$ (uniqueness of successors)

3. $R000$

4. $\forall x\, \forall y\, \forall z\, [(Sxy \wedge S0z) \rightarrow (Rx00 \rightarrow Ryz0)]$

5. $\forall x\, \forall y\, \forall u\, \forall v\, \forall w\, \forall z\, [(Suy \wedge Sxv \wedge S0w \wedge Swz) \rightarrow (Rx0u \rightarrow Rvzy)]$

6. $\forall x\, \forall y\, \forall z\, \forall w\, [(S0z \wedge Szw) \rightarrow (\neg Rxzy \vee \neg Rxwy)]$

Lines 1 and 2 say explicitly about the successor relation what went without saying about the successor function because existence and uniqueness of values of functions are wired into the tree rules. Lines 3 through 6 correspond to the old-style sentences in the box of Figure 8.1. In line 4 the antecedent "$(Sxy \wedge S0z)$" of the main conditional identifies y as $x + 1$ and z as 1, so that the consequent, "$(Rx00 \rightarrow Ryz0)$," says what "$(Rx00 \rightarrow Rsxs00)$" did in Figure 8.1. In line 5 the same device is used at greater length to identify y as $u + 1$, v as $x + 1$ and z as 2, where before "su," "sx," and "$ss0$" were used.

If we had begun with associated sets of sentences of this sort, the proof of Section 8.3 would have proceeded as before, with slight adjustments to accommodate the changed notation. The result would have been a reduction of the halting problem to decision problem III. Note that except for the first premise (existence of successors) all sentences in the new associated set are of the $\forall$ form; without that premise the set would meet the conditions of type II above, and the tree test would terminate after some finite number of steps whether or not the program halted.

Thus the class of new-style associated arguments misses decidability only because of the presence in each of them of the insidious premise "$\forall x\, \exists y\, Sxy$," endlessly generating new names.

8.7 UNDECIDABILITY OF TWO-PLACE PREDICATE LOGIC

IV. Unsolvable: the decision problem for consistency of finite sets of sentences without names or function symbols in which all predicates have exactly two places.

The work of the single $(n + 2)$ place predicate "R" can be done by $n + 1$ different two-place ("binary") predicates—say, "T," "A," "B," ..., which are to be interpreted as follows:

Txy: at time x we traverse arrow y.

Axz: at time x there are z stones in register A.

Bxw: at time x there are w stones in register B.

The treatment in Section 8.7 is again due to George Boolos.

and so on, so that (with $n = 2$) "$Rxyzw$" can be replaced by the conjunction of the foregoing three. The work of the name "0" can be done by a two-place predicate "Z," which is to be interpreted as follows:

$$Zxy: (x = 0 \land y = y)$$

Clearly the second place is vacuous; with "Z" interpreted so, any one of the following will serve as a way of saying that $x = 0$.

$$\forall y\, Zxy \qquad \exists y\, Zxy \qquad Zxx$$

Now we can convert new-style arguments into newer-style arguments, in which no names or function symbols occur, and in which all predicate symbols have two places. The undecidability proof outlined in Section 8.6 is readily adapted to type IV.

8.8 PROBLEMS

1. *A solvable decision problem.* A sentence is in *prenex* form when all its quantifiers (if any) are at the extreme left. An "$\forall\exists$" sentence is one in prenex form with any universal quantifiers left of any existential ones. "$\forall\exists$" sentences are the other way around, with any existential quantifiers at the left. Prove the following.* There is a solution at the back of the book.

> V. Solvable: the decision problem for validity of arguments with no function symbols in which all premises have $\exists\forall$ form and the conclusion has $\forall\exists$ form.

2. *New-style associated sets of sentences.* Write these out for the programs of Figure 7.9.

3. *Equivalence.* Show by the tree method that in the presence of the additional premises

$$\forall x\, \exists y\, Sxy \text{ (existence)} \qquad \forall x\, \forall y\, \forall z\, [(Sxy \land Sxz) \to y = z] \text{ (uniqueness)}$$

each of the following implies the other:

$$\forall x\, (Sax \to Sxb) \qquad \exists y\, (Sax \land Sxb)$$

4. *Project.* Modify the proof (Section 8.3) that the associated argument is valid iff the program halts, to make it work for the new-style associated arguments that use "S" and "$=$."

5. *Project.* Repeat problem 4 for the newer-style associated arguments that use only two-place predicate symbols "Z," "T," "A," etc., and use no names or function symbols.

---

* *Hint*: See the proof of II.

9

INCOMPLETENESS

We now extend the logical system of Chapters 1 through 8, and prove the following version of Kurt Gödel's famous incompleteness theorem of 1931: For the extended system there can be no sound, complete clerical routine for recognizing validity. We'll do that by reducing the decision problem for first-order validity (Chapter 8) to the problem of designing such a routine.

9.1 SECOND-ORDER LOGIC

It's "first-order" logic for which the tree test was proved sound and complete in Chapters 2 through 6. Second-order logic is what first-order logic becomes when we allow universal and existential quantification of predicate letters, as in the sentence

$$\forall x \, \forall y \, [x = y \leftrightarrow \forall P \, (Px \to Py)]$$

according to which identity of individuals is definable as possession by one of them of every property that the other possesses, and in the sentence

$$\forall x \, \forall y \, \exists R \, Rxy$$

according to which any two things are related somehow or other. In these sentences the letter "P" is used as a one-place predicate variable, for properties of individuals, and the letter "R" is used as a two-place predicate variable, for relations between individuals. Another example is the sentence

$$\forall P \, \{[P0 \,\wedge\, \forall x \, (Px \to Psx)] \to \forall x \, Px\}$$

viz., the axiom of mathematical *induction*, according to which (in its intended interpretation) anything true of 0 and of the successors of the things it's true of is true of everything in the domain of the variable "x." In second-order logic we can also quantify function symbols, as in the generalization

$$\exists z \, \exists f \, \forall P \, \{[Pz \,\wedge\, \forall x \, (Px \to Pfx)] \to \forall x \, Px\}$$

of the induction axiom, viz., the axiom of *enumerability*, which will reappear in our proof of Gödel's incompleteness theorem as part of an axiom of *enumerable infinity*.

We can apply the tree method to second-order reasoning—reasoning that involves second-order sentences—as soon as we know what is meant by an instance of a predicate variable. To see what that must mean, let's apply the tree test for logical truth to the second-order definition of identity displayed above. We get so far without applying UI or EI to "P":

1    $\checkmark \, \neg \forall x \, \forall y \, [x = y \leftrightarrow \forall P \, (Px \to Py)]$

2    $\checkmark \, \exists x \, \neg \forall y \, [x = y \leftrightarrow \forall P \, (Px \to Py)]$ (from 1)

3    $\checkmark \, \neg \forall y \, [a = y \leftrightarrow \forall P \, (Pa \to Py)]$ (from 2)

4    $\checkmark \, \exists y \, \neg [a = y \leftrightarrow \forall P \, (Pa \to Py)]$ (from 3)

5    $\checkmark \, \neg [a = b \leftrightarrow \forall P \, (Pa \to Pb)]$ (from 4)

6    $a = b$ $\neg a = b$ (from 5)

7    $\checkmark \, \neg \forall P \, (Pa \to Pb)$ $\forall P \, (Pa \to Pb)$ (from 5)

8    $\exists P \, \neg (Pa \to Pb)$ (from 7)

Now it's easy enough to apply EI to line 8; all we need is a one-place predicate constant, new to the path. As no predicate constants at all appear in the path, any one will do—say, "K." Then the left-hand path closes:

8    $\checkmark \, \exists P \, \neg (Pa \to Pb)$

9    $\checkmark \, \neg (Ka \to Kb)$ (from 8 by EI)

10   Ka (from 9)

11    $\neg Kb$ (from 9)

12   Kb (from 6, 10 by =)

×

The right-hand path also closes if, in applying UI to "$\forall P\ (Pa \to Pb)$" at the right of line 7, we denote the instance of the predicate variable "P" by the expression "$a=$," i.e., choose the particular property of *being a* as our instance of "P":

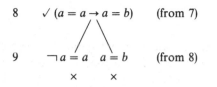

8    $\checkmark\ (a = a \to a = b)$ (from 7)

9    $\neg a = a$ $a = b$ (from 8)

Then the tree closes; the sentence is a logical truth. Then in second-order logic we can get along without the sign of identity, writing "$\forall P\ (Px \to Py)$" to the same effect as "$x = y$."

In this particular example we were able to use an instance of "P" for which there was a handy expression "$a=$" that acted like a predicate constant; we just slotted it in for "P" in "$Pa \to Pb$" to get a line "$(a = a \to a = b)$" that made the tree close in two more steps. But that was just luck. In other cases the required instance won't be a property for which our notation provides anything that acts like a predicate constant. An example is provided by the test for logical truth of the claim that individuals (or an individual) named "a" and "b" stand in some relation to each other (or itself). It starts like this:

1    $\checkmark \neg \exists R\ Rab$

2    $\forall R \neg Rab$ (from 1 by EI)

Now line 2 is false, because in any interpretation, a and b must stand in the relation $=$ of identity or $\neq$ of diversity depending on whether or not that interpretation assigns "a" and "b" the same extension. This relation of identity-or-diversity isn't expressible in our notation in the way the property of "being a" was, for we can't just write "$(= \vee \neq)$" in place of "R" and get a sentence; "$(= \vee \neq)ab$" is gibberish. Still, given any names "a" and "b," we can write out a sentence "$(a = b \vee a \neq b)$" in our notation, saying that the particular individuals a and b do stand in the relation identity or diversity. Thus we can write the required instance of line 2 as

3    $\neg (a = b \vee a \neq b)$ (from 2 by UI)

The tree now closes via the truth-functional rule of Chapter 2.

In the first example of UI the extension of the instantial predicate in any interpretation was the set whose only member is the extension of "a" in that interpretation; in the second example it was the set of all pairs of individuals in the interpretation's domain, since one or the other of the relations " $=$ " and " $\neq$ " must hold between any i and any j. In any case it's routine to write out sentences like "$(a = a \rightarrow a = b)$" and "$(a = b \lor a \neq b)$" in our notation that express the result of applying UI, even when we can find no predicate constant like "$a=$" with the right extension.

9.2 PROBLEMS

By the tree method, show that identity is transitive and symmetrical according to the second-order definition given above, i.e., show that the following arguments are valid:

1. $\forall P (Pa \rightarrow Pb)$, $\forall P (Pb \rightarrow Pc)$, so $\forall P (Pa \rightarrow Pc)$
2. $\forall P (Pa \rightarrow Pb)$, so $\forall P (Pb \rightarrow Pa)$

9.3 LOGICAL TYPES

Properties of individuals can have properties too, viz., second-level properties. Notable examples are the properties of being true of nothing at all, being true of exactly one individual, being true of exactly two individuals, etc. The property C of being a centaur has the first of these second-level properties, for which we use the symbol "0":

$$0C \leftrightarrow \neg \exists x \; Cx$$

The property D of being the current Dalai Lama has the second of these second-level properties, which we'll call "1":

$$1D \leftrightarrow \exists x \; \forall y \; (Dy \leftrightarrow x = y)$$

And the property E of being a planet closer than the Earth to the sun has the third of these second-level properties:

$$2E \leftrightarrow \exists x \; \exists y \; \{x \neq y \; \land \; \forall z \; [Ez \leftrightarrow (z = x \; \lor \; z = y)]\}$$

That's how Gottlob Frege analyzed the natural numbers 0, 1, 2, etc.[*]

The term "higher-order logic" refers to a hierarchy that has a bottom, 0th level, but has no top: see Table 9.1. The items at level 0 are simply the individuals in the domain over which the familiar variables "x," "y," etc., range. The term "individuals" is meant to be a neutral designation for whatever items may have been assigned to the ground level—even if these are items like schools of fish that might be thought of as sets of individuals, or items like cardinal numbers that might be thought of as properties of properties. It is with that understanding that we speak of "x" and "y" as individual variables, and of names "a" and "b" as individual constants.

---

[*] *Grundgesetze der Arithmetik*, vol. 1, Jena, 1893. Translation and commentary by Montgomery Furth, *The Basic Laws of Arithmetic*, University of California Press, Berkeley and Los Angeles, 1964.

TABLE 9.1
Hierarchy of logical types

Level 3:	Properties/relations of items at levels 0, 1, 2
Level 2:	Properties/relations of items at levels 0, 1
Level 1:	Properties/relations of items at level 0
Level 0:	Individuals

Those variables and constants belong to level 0. To level 1 belong variables like "P" and constants like "$=$," "C," "D," and "E" above. And the predicates "0," "1," "2" defined above are third-level constants—relative to the level 0 of items they are thought to be properties of properties of. But of course in theories like Robinson arithmetic we are free to choose the set of natural numbers as the domain, over which the individual variables range, even if we follow Frege's analysis: the domain of individuals can be any nonempty set we choose, and the higher levels are determined by that choice.

Example. In an interpretation where the domain of individuals is the set of all natural numbers, where the extension of the first-level predicate constant "A" is the set of numbers that are equal to their own squares, and where the second-level predicate constant "2" is defined as above, the sentence "$2A$" is true.

It was Bertrand Russell[*] who proposed the system of levels, together with the following restriction.

> **Type restriction.** When one symbol is predicted of another, the former must belong to a higher level ("type") than the latter.

Thus, since the constants "1," "$=$," "D" belong to levels 2, 1, 1, and the variables "x" and "y" belong to level 0, Russell's type restriction is satisfied when we write

$$1D \leftrightarrow \exists x \, \forall y \, (Dy \leftrightarrow x = y)$$

In Frege's formalization[†] of logic, where no such restriction is imposed, paradoxes arise. The simplest of these was discovered by Russell in 1901.[‡]

---

[*] "Mathematical Logic as Based on the Theory of Types," *American Journal of Mathematics*, **30**: 222–262, 1908.

[†] Gottlob Frege, *Begriffsschrift*, Halle, 1879. Translated in Jean van Heijenoort (ed.), *From Frege to Gödel*, Harvard University Press, Cambridge, Mass., 1967.

[‡] See "Letter to Frege" in Jean van Heijenoort, op. cit., pp. 124–125.

9.4   RUSSELL'S PARADOX

Plausibly, Frege assumed that any condition that can be formulated determines a predicate, applicable to the things that satisfy the condition. For example, the condition

$$\neg\, \exists x\; Lvx$$

is met by the people v who love no one. Unaware of the need for a type restriction, Frege would have formulated the assumption that this condition determines a predicate w as follows:

$$\exists w\; \forall v\; (wv \leftrightarrow \neg\, \exists x\; Lvx)$$

That assumption is quite natural and harmless. And in general it may seem harmless and natural to make the following assumption, where ...v... is any condition on v:

Comprehension axiom. $\exists w\; \forall v\; (wv \leftrightarrow ...v...)$

But not all sentences of that form are true. Thus, suppose that ...v... is the condition

$$\neg\, vv$$

of non-self-applicability. For example, "Loves somebody" is a non-self-applicable condition, for it is people, not conditions, that love. Then non-self-applicability may seem to be a genuine condition, determining a predicate w according to the comprehension axiom. But as Russell pointed out in a letter to Frege in 1902, a contradiction arises when we make that assumption.

> Let w be the predicate: to be a predicate that cannot be predicated of itself. Can w be predicated of itself? From each answer its opposite follows. Therefore we must conclude that w is not a predicate.

In other words, when we put the condition "$\neg\, vv$" for "...v..." in the comprehension axiom, we obtain a sentence

$$\exists w\; \forall v\; (wv \leftrightarrow \neg\, vv)$$

that cannot be true, for it is inconsistent, as the following tree test shows:

1   ✓ $\exists w\ \forall v\ (wv \leftrightarrow \neg\, vv)$ (Consistent?)

2      $\forall v\ (av \leftrightarrow \neg\, vv)$ (from 1)

3   ✓ $(aa \leftrightarrow \neg\, aa)$ (from 2)

4   aa $\neg\, aa$ (from 3)

5     $\neg\, aa$ aa (from 3)

         ×   ×

Thus Frege's system is inconsistent in the absence of some such restriction as Russell's on the condition $\ldots v \ldots$ in the comprehension axiom.

9.5 SECOND-ORDER FORMATION AND VALUATION RULES

First-order logic allows for zeroth-level (individual) constants and variables and for first-level (predicate and function) constants but not for first-level variables. In general, $(n + 1)$-order logic allows for constants and variables of levels 0 through n, and for constants but not variables of level $(n + 1)$. Thus, second-order logic can use quantifiers "$\forall P$," "$\exists P$," "$\forall Q$," etc., where "P," "Q," etc., are variables for predicates, and quantifiers "$\forall f$," "$\exists f$," "$\forall g$," etc., where "f" and "g" are variables for functions, as well as individual quantifiers "$\forall x$," "$\exists x$," "$\forall y$," etc.

We count all first-order sentences as second-order sentences as well, and get further second-order sentences by rewriting predicate constants and function constants as variables and then quantifying. For example, replace the predicate constant "K" by the variable "R" and existentially generalize, to turn the sentence:

Alma knows no one who loves the Baron. $\forall x\ (Lxb \to \neg\, Kax)$

into a weaker, second-order sentence:

There is a relation that Alma bears to no one who loves the Baron.

$$\exists R\ \forall x(Lxb \to \neg\, Rax)$$

Another example is provided by the second-order sentence that asserts the existence of a function f and an individual x having the properties that the first two axioms ($Q1$, $Q2$) of Robinson arithmetic attribute to the successor function s and the number 0:

$$\exists z\ \exists f\ [\forall x\ \forall y\ (x \neq y \to fx \neq fy) \wedge \forall x\ z \neq fx]$$

We can now convert the rules of formation for first-order logic into rules of formation for second-order logic simply by adding the following to the formation rules of Chapters 4, 5, and 6.

Formation. All first-order sentences are second-order sentences too. If $\ldots K \ldots$ is a second-order sentence in which the n-place predicate constant K of first order appears but the n-place predicate variable R of first order does not, both $\forall R \ldots R \ldots$ and $\exists R \ldots R \ldots$ are second-order sentences. Similarly for functions: if $\ldots k \ldots$ is a second-order sentence in which the n-place function constant k of first order appears but the n-place function variable f of first order does not, both $\forall f \ldots f \ldots$ and $\exists f \ldots f \ldots$ are second-order sentences.

Thus "$\forall x\,(Lxb \to \neg\,Kax)$" counts as a second-order sentence, and so does "$\exists R\,\forall x\,(Lxb \to \neg\,Rax)$," where "$R$" is a two-place predicate variable.

The rules of valuation of second-order logic are the six valuation rules of first-order logic taken over wholesale together with one more, the counterpart of the foregoing rule of formation.

Valuation. Given that K is an n-place first-order predicate letter to which an interpretation C assigns no extension; that C_S is like C except for assigning an extension S to K (i.e., a set S of n-tuples of individuals in the domain of C); and that K does not appear in $\ldots R \ldots$:

7a. A sentence of form $\forall R \ldots R \ldots$ is true or false in C depending on whether or not $\ldots K \ldots$ is true in every interpretation of form C_S.

7b. A sentence of form $\exists R \ldots R \ldots$ is true or false in C depending on whether or not $\ldots K \ldots$ is true in some interpretation of form C_S.

This case is similar for n-place first-order function letters, with "k" and "f" in place of "K" and "R," and in place of S, an n-place function defined for all arguments in C's domain and assigning all its values in C's domain.

9.6   MATHEMATICAL INDUCTION

The axiom of mathematical induction is a second-order sentence true in the intended interpretation of Robinson arithmetic that can be added to the axioms of that theory to get a set of axioms from which second-order sentences follow logically iff true in that interpretation:*

---

* The proof (along the lines of the categoricity proof in Section 9.7) is straightforward; see George Boolos and Richard Jeffrey, *Computability and Logic*, Cambridge University Press, 3rd ed., 1989, chap. 18.

> *Induction axiom.* $\forall P \ \{[P0 \ \wedge \ \forall x \ (Px \to Psx)] \to \forall x \ Px\}$

This sentence says that anything true of 0 and of the successors of all the things it's true of is true of everything in the domain. If the sentence is true in an interpretation I, then the endless list "0," "$s0$," "$ss0$," ... (in which each entry after the first is obtained by writing one more "s" than in the preceding entry) enumerates the whole domain of I—perhaps with repetitions.*

> *Enumerability.* The interpretations in which the induction axiom is true are those in which the list $0, s0, ss0, sss0, \ldots$ enumerates the whole domain.

Axiom Q3 of Robinson arithmetic, "$\forall x \ (x \neq 0 \to \exists y \ x = sy),$" is deducible from the induction axiom. This is shown by the tree test below, in which we use the following style of abbreviation: "$Z(x)$" is short for "$(x \neq 0 \to \exists y \ x = sy).$" Thus, written out in full, the left-hand side of line 5 below is "$\neg (0 \neq 0 \to \exists y \ 0 = sy),$" and line 9 is "$\neg (sa \neq 0 \to \exists y \ sa = sy).$" The tree closes:

1	$\forall P \ (\{P0 \ \wedge \ \forall x \ [Px \to Psx]\} \to \forall x \ Px)$	(premise)
2	$\neg \forall x \ Z(x)$	($\neg$ conclusion)
3	$\checkmark \ \{Z(0) \ \wedge \ \forall x \ [Z(x) \to Z(sx)]\} \to \forall x \ Z(x)$	(from 1 by UI)

4	$\checkmark \ \neg \{Z(0) \ \wedge \ \forall x \ [Z(x) \to Z(sx)]\}$	$\forall x \ Z(x)$	(from 3)
		$\times$	
5	$\checkmark \ \neg Z(0)$ $\qquad$ $\checkmark \ \neg \forall x \ [Z(x) \to Z(sx)]$		(from 4)
6	$0 \neq 0$ $\qquad\qquad$ $\checkmark \ \exists y \ \neg [Z(x) \to Z(sx)]$		(from 5)
7	$\times$ $\qquad\qquad\quad$ $\checkmark \ \neg [Z(a) \to Z(sa)]$		(from 6)
8	$Z(a)$		(from 7)
9	$\checkmark \ \neg Z(sa)$		(from 7)
10	$sa \neq 0$		(from 9)
11	$\checkmark \ \neg \exists y \ sa = xy$		(from 9)
12	$\forall y \ sa \neq sy$		(from 11)
13	$sa \neq sa$		(from 12)
	$\times$		

---

* *Proof.* Where P is the property of being the extension in I of a name on the list, "$P0$" and "$\forall x \ (Px \to Psx)$" are both true in I. Then if the induction axiom is true in I, so will be "$\forall x \ Px,$" a sentence saying that every individual in the domain is named in the list.

9.7 ISOMORPHISM, CATEGORICITY, COMPLETENESS

The induction axiom is true in all four of the interpretations of "*s*" and "0" shown in Figure 9.1. It follows that the axiom is not *categorical*, i.e., it doesn't require that the interpretations of "*s*" and "0" in which it is true have graphs that are convertible into each other simply by relabeling nodes. Such interpretations are called *isomorphic* (Greek, "same shape"). Isomorphic interpretations always agree in the truth values they assign to sentences. For the record, here are the definitions:

> A set of axioms is said to be **categorical** when any two interpretations in which they are all true are **isomorphic** to each other, i.e., the same graph serves for both, except perhaps for the labeling of nodes.

The four graphs in Figure 9.1 can't be converted into each other by relabeling nodes, for they have different numbers of nodes: 1, 2, 3, infinity. But if we add two more axioms (Q1, Q2) as below, the resulting set ZS of axioms of the second-order theory of zero and successor will prove to be categorical.

> **The Axioms ZS**
> $\forall P \{[P0 \land \forall x (Px \to Psx)] \to \forall x\, Px\}$ (Induction)
> $\forall x\, \forall y\, (x \neq y \to sx \neq sy)$ (Q1)
> $\forall x\, 0 \neq sx$ (Q2)

With reference to Figure 9.1, Q1 is false in interpretations like that of (*c*), where distinct individuals (0 and *j*) have the same successor (*i*). Q2 is false in interpretations like (*a*) and (*b*), where 0 is a successor, whether of itself as in (*a*) or of some other individual as in (*b*). The sort of interpretations that the induction axiom itself rules out are illustrated by the nonstandard interpretation of problem 2 in Section 6.10, where some individuals (*i*, *j*) aren't accessible from 0 by any finite number of applications of the successor operation (the arrows of Figure 9.2).

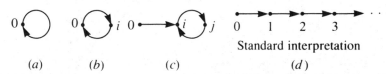

Standard interpretation

(*a*)   (*b*)   (*c*)   (*d*)

FIGURE 9.1
Noncategoricity of the axiom of mathematical induction. (Arrows go from *x* to *sx*.)

0   1   2   3

FIGURE 9.2
Mathematical induction is false in this interpretation.

> *Categoricity of ZS.* Any interpretation I in which Q1, Q2, and induction are all true is isomorphic to the intended interpretation N.

Proof. Since the induction axiom implies enumerability (Section 9.6), we know that the domain of I is exhaustively enumerated by the list "0," "s0," "ss0," etc. Axiom Q2 tells us that in I the extension of the first entry, "0," is the extension of no name later in the list: $0 \neq s0$, $0 \neq ss0$, $0 \neq sss0$, etc. Q1 then implies that different names in the list (with different numbers of esses) must have different extensions in I, e.g., "$ss0 = sssss0$" can't be true in I because if it were, then by two applications of Q1 as in problem 1*b* of Section 5.10, "$0 = sss0$" would be true in I, and so Q2 would be false in I. Then the names "0," "s0," "ss0," etc., all have different extensions in I, and the extension of "s" in I is a function that assigns to the extension of each listed name as argument the extension of the next name in the list as value. This description remains true if we replace "I" by "N" throughout, so the two interpretations are isomorphic.

Table 9.2 displays the isomorphism in the case of a particular offbeat interpretation I, in which the extension of the name "0" is the number 1, the extension of "s" is the function "one tenth of," and the domain is the set $\{1, .1, .01, .001, \ldots\}$.

TABLE 9.2
Extensions in two interpretations of ZS

Name:	"0"	"s0"	"ss0"	"sss0"	"ssss0"	etc.
Extension in N:	0	1	2	3	4	etc.
Extension in I:	1	1/10	1/100	1/1,000	1/10,000	etc.

From the categoricity of ZS it follows that Q1, Q2, and induction provide a complete characterization of the natural numbers and the successor function, in the following sense. (Clearly, this sort of completeness— of a set of axioms, relative to an interpretation—is not the same thing as completeness of a routine method for recognizing validity.)

> **Completeness of ZS as a characterization of N.** The argument "ZS, so $\bigcirc$" is valid *iff* $\bigcirc$ is true in the intended interpretation N.

Proof. "only if." Any sentence $\bigcirc$ implied by Q1, Q2, and induction is true in all interpretations in which those axioms are all true; as N is such an interpretation, $\bigcirc$ will be true in N.

Proof: " if." If $\bigcirc$ is true in N, then it is true in any interpretation isomorphic to N; so by categoricity of ZS, $\bigcirc$ will be true in every interpretation where Q1, Q2, and induction are all true.

9.8 INCOMPLETENESS OF VALIDITY TESTS FOR SECOND-ORDER LOGIC

We now prove Gödel's theorem (1931) on the nonexistence of sound, complete routines for recognizing validity of arbitrary arguments in the notation of second-order logic. (The numeration continues from Chapter 8.)

VI. Unsolvable: the problem of designing a sound, complete clerical routine for recognizing second-order validity.

Of course it's not the logic that's incomplete, but the tests for validity. As we shall see, the theorem follows from the nonexistence proved in Chapter 8 of sound, complete routines for detecting first-order *invalidity* (and consistency), together with the existence we shall now demonstrate of a routine method that can be applied to arbitrary first-order sentences to find second-order arguments that are valid iff the first-order sentences are consistent.

Crucial to this demonstration is the following fact, first proved by Leopold Löwenheim in 1915.

Löwenheim's theorem. If a first-order sentence is consistent, it is true in some interpretation with an enumerable domain.

Proof. The theorem follows easily from the tree method's soundness as a test for consistency of first-order sentences: If a first-order sentence is consistent, the tree constructed according to the flowchart of Figure 6.1 will never close, and each never-closing path in it will determine an interpretation in which the sentence is true. The domain of that interpretation is enumerable, being enumerated by the list of names occurring in that path, names which, translated into the notation of Robinson arithmetic, would be some of or all the names in the endless list "0," "$s0$," "$ss0$," etc.

To prove Gödel's incompleteness theorem it is now shown that any routine positive test for second-order validity would provide something that we learned in Chapter 8 does not exist—a routine positive test for consistency of arbitrary first-order sentences.

The idea is that by Löwenheim's theorem consistency of a first-order sentence comes to the same thing as truth in some interpretation with an enumerable domain, i.e., a domain that can be paired off one to one with some set of natural numbers. Now we can get a second-order sentence that's true in exactly the interpretations whose domains can be paired off one to one with the set of *all* the natural numbers—the *enumerably infinite* domains—by conjoining the three axioms of ZS and existentially generalizing the name "0" and the function symbol "*s*." Call the result "EInf."

The following sentence **EInF** is true or false in interpretations depending on whether or not their domains are enumerably infinite.

$$\exists f\, \exists z\, (\forall x\, z \neq fx \;\wedge\; \forall x\, \forall y\, (fx = fy \to x = y) \;\wedge$$
$$\forall P\{[Pz \;\wedge\; \forall x(Px \to Pfx)] \to \forall x\, Px\})$$

Note that the truth value of EInf in an interpretation I depends in no way on the extensions that I assigns to names, predicate letters, and function symbols; it depends only on the size of I's domain.

Now for any sentence ◯ of first-order logic—say, the sentence "$\forall x\, \exists y\, Lxsy$"—and a new one-place predicate constant "D" (for "domain"), we define the relativization of ◯ to D as follows:

The **relativization** of ◯ to D is the result ("◯/D") of carrying out operations 1 through 4:

1. Replace each occurrence of "$\exists x...$" in ◯ by an occurrence of "$\exists x\, (Dx \;\wedge\; ...)$"—and follow a similar procedure for other variables.
2. Replace each occurrence of "$\forall x...$" in ◯ by an occurrence of "$\forall x\, (Dx \to ...)$"—and follow a similar procedure for other variables.
3. For each letter name in ◯ (say, "a") conjoin "Da" to ◯, and if there are no letter names, conjoin "$\exists x\, Dx$."
4. For each n-place function symbol in ◯ (say, "s," with $n = 1$) conjoin "$\forall x\, (Dx \to Dsx)$" to ◯.

Where ◯ is "$\forall x\, \exists y\, Lxsy$," the cumulative results of applying operations 1 through 4 in order are as follows:

1. $\forall x\, \exists y\, (Dy \;\wedge\; Lxsy)$
2. $\forall x\, [Dx \to \exists y\, (Dy \;\wedge\; Lxsy)]$
3. $\forall x\, [Dx \to \exists y\, (Dy \;\wedge\; Lxsy)] \;\wedge\; \exists x\, Dx$
4. ◯/D = "$\forall x\, [Dx \to \exists y\, (Dy \;\wedge\; Lxsy)] \;\wedge\; \exists x\, Dx \;\wedge\; \forall x\, (Dx \to Dsx)$"

In an interpretation in which the sentence $\bigcirc = $ "$\forall x \, \exists y \, Lxsy$" says that every natural number is less than the successor of some natural number, the three conjuncts of the sentence $\bigcirc/D$ say that every natural number with the property D is less than the successor of some natural number with property D, that some natural number does have property D, and that the successors of natural numbers with property D also have property D.

By the *existential generalization* of a first-order sentence—say, "$\forall x \, \exists y \, Lxsy$"—we shall mean the second-order sentence—here, "$\exists R \, \exists f \, \forall x \, \exists y \, Rxfy$"—obtained by replacing all nonlogical constants by new variables, which are then existentially quantified. The nonlogical constants are the names, function symbols, and predicate constants except for the sign "I" or "$=$" of identity, which we regard as a logical constant. Thus, the existential generalization of "$\forall x \, x = a$" is "$\exists y \, \forall x \, x = y$."

$EG(\bigcirc)$ is the result of replacing all nonlogical constants in $\bigcirc$ by new variables and existentially generalizing the result.

Where $\bigcirc$ is "$\forall x \, \exists y \, Lxsy$" the constants in $\bigcirc/D$ as above are "D," "L," "s." To get $EG(\bigcirc/D)$ we replace these by variables "Q," "R," "f" and existentially generalize the result:

$$EG(\bigcirc/D) = \text{"}\exists Q \, \exists R \, \exists f \, \{\forall x \, [Qx \to \exists y \, (Qy \land Rxfy)]$$

$$\land \, \exists x \, Qx \land \forall x \, (Qx \to Qfx)\}\text{"}$$

According to the rules of valuation for "$\exists$," the sentence $EG(\bigcirc/D)$ will be true in an interpretation I iff some nonempty subset of I's domain is the domain of an interpretation in which the sentence $\bigcirc$ is true. As there are no constants in $EG(\bigcirc/D)$, its truth value in I depends only on the size of I's domain, and not on the particular individuals that compose it or on the extensions I assigns to names, predicate constants, and function constants.

Reduction theorem. A first-order sentence $\bigcirc$ is consistent iff the second-order argument "EInf, so $EG(\bigcirc/D)$" is valid.

Proof: "only if." By Löwenheim's theorem, $\bigcirc$ is consistent iff it is true in some interpretation with an enumerable domain, a domain that's part of some enumerably infinite set. Then $\bigcirc$ is consistent iff $EG(\bigcirc/D)$ is true in some interpretation with an enumerably infinite domain and, therefore (since no constants appear in it), in every interpretation with an enumerably infinite domain. The sentence EInf is true in exactly the interpretations that have enumerably infinite domains. Then if $\bigcirc$ is consistent, $EG(\bigcirc/D)$ is true in all interpretations in which EInf is true; the argument "EInf, so $EG(\bigcirc/D)$" is valid.

Proof: "if." If the argument "EInf, so $EG(\bigcirc/D)$" is valid, $EG(\bigcirc/D)$ is true in every interpretation in which EInf is true, i.e., every interpretation with an enumerably infinite domain. Thus for some enumerable set D that isn't empty, $\bigcirc$ is true in some interpretation with domain D. Then $\bigcirc$ is consistent.

This proves the reduction theorem. It follows that a sound, complete general routine for testing validity of second-order arguments would also be a sound, complete general routine for testing consistency of first-order sentences (and invalidity of first-order arguments with finite numbers of premises), thus solving the decision problem for first-order logic, which we know to be unsolvable. (Note that consistency of a finite set of sentences comes to the same thing as consistency of the conjunction of the sentences in the set, i.e., a single sentence $\bigcirc$ as in the reduction theorem.)

9.9 PROBLEMS

The reduction theorem can be simplified, both in general (1 and 2 below) and in special cases (3). Modify its proof so as to establish the following. There are hints at the back of the book.

1. A first-order sentence $\bigcirc$ is consistent iff the second-order argument "Q1, Q2, induction, so $EG(\bigcirc/D)$" is valid.
2. A first-order sentence $\bigcirc$ is consistent iff the second-order argument "Q1, Q2, so $EG(\bigcirc/D)$" is valid.
3. A first-order sentence $\bigcirc$ that doesn't contain the sign of identity is consistent iff the second-order argument "Q1, Q2, induction, so $EG(\bigcirc)$" is valid.

9.10 SOME HISTORY

Logic came of age in the years 1930–1931, with Gödel's completeness and incompleteness theorems.

The system for which he proved completeness in 1930 was a cleaned-up version of the system of first-order logic in volume 1 of Bertrand Russell's and Alfred North Whitehead's monumental joint work *Principia Mathematica* (Cambridge University Press, 1910, 1925). The cleaning up had been done by David Hilbert and Wilhelm Ackermann in *Grundzüge der theoretischen Logik* (Springer, Berlin, 1928). (The tree method for which we proved completeness at the ends of Chapters 2 through 6 does the same job, but is much easier to use and to prove complete.) Here is the beginning of Gödel's 1930 paper:

> Whitehead and Russell, as is well known, constructed logic and mathematics by initially taking certain evident propositions as axioms and deriving the theorems of logic and mathematics from these by means of some precisely formulated principles of inference in a purely formal way (that is, without making further use of the meaning of the symbols). Of course, when such a

procedure is followed the question at once arises whether the initially postulated system of axioms and principles of inference is complete, that is, whether it actually suffices for the derivation of *every* logico-mathematical proposition, or whether, perhaps, it is conceivable that there are true propositions (which may even be provable by means of other principles) that cannot be derived in the system under consideration. For the formulas of the propositional calculus the question has been settled affirmatively; that is, it has been shown that every correct formula of the propositional calculus does indeed follow from the axioms given in *Principia Mathematica*. The same will be done here for a wider realm of formulas, namely, those of the "restricted functional calculus"; that is, we shall prove Theorem I. *Every valid formula of the restricted functional calculus is provable.**

(Valid formula = correct formula = logical truth; propositional calculus = a routine for recognizing truth-functional logical truth; restricted functional calculus = a routine for recognizing first-order logical truth.)

Gödel's completeness theorem of 1930 had the effect of demonstrating the adequacy of an existing formalization of a large portion of the logic used in mathematical reasoning. The incompleteness theorem published in the following year was quite another matter, a proof that beyond first-order logic our reach may be expected to exceed our grasp. Here is the beginning of the 1931 paper:

> The development of mathematics toward greater precision has led, as is well known, to the formalization of large tracts of it, so that one can prove any theorem using nothing but a few mechanical rules. The most comprehensive formal systems that have been set up hitherto are the system of *Principia Mathematica* (*PM*) on the one hand and the Zermelo-Fraenkel system of set theory (further developed by J. von Neumann) on the other. These two systems are so comprehensive that in them all methods of proof today used in mathematics are formalized, that is, reduced to a few axioms and rules of inference. One might therefore conjecture that these axioms and rules of inference are sufficient to decide *any* mathematical question that can at all be formally expressed in these systems. It will be shown below that this is not the case, that on the contrary there are in the two systems mentioned relatively simple problems in the theory of integers that cannot be decided on the basis of the axioms. This situation is not in any way due to the special nature of the systems that have been set up but holds for a wide class of formal sytems....†

---

* "Die Vollständigkeit der Axiome des logischen Funktionenkalküls," *Monatshefte für Mathematik und Physik*, **37**: 349–360, 1930, as translated in Kurt Gödel, *Collected Works*, vol. I, Solomon Feferman et al., eds., Oxford University Press, New York, Clarendon Press, Oxford, 1986, pp. 103–123, "The Completeness of the Axioms of the Functional Calculus of Logic."

† Über formal unenscheidbare Sätze der Principia mathematica und verwandter Systeme I," *Monatshefte für Mathematik und Physik*, **38**: 173–198, 1931, as translated in Gödel, op. cit. (previqus footnote), pp. 145–195, "On Formally Undecidable Propositions of *Principia Mathematica* and Related Systems I."

Exactly how wide a class of formal systems? In 1936 Alan Turing answered that question to Gödel's satisfaction, as Gödel testifies in a brief addendum to the English translation of his 1931 paper:

> In consequence of later advances, in particular of the fact that due to A. N. Turing's work a precise and unquestionably adequate definition of the general notion of formal system can now be given, a completely general version of theorems VI and XI is now possible. That is, it can be proved rigorously that in *every* consistent formal system that contains a certain amount of finitary number theory there exist undecidable arithmetic propositions and that, moreover, the consistency of any such system cannot be proved in the system.*

These theorems, which go beyond theorem VI of Section 9.8, have profound significance for the practice and the philosophy of mathematics.†

---

* Gödel, op. cit. (previous footnote), p. 191. Turing's paper is "On Computable Numbers, with an Application to the Entscheidungsproblem," *Proceedings of the London Mathematical Society*, series 2, **42**: 230–262, 1936–1937; corrections *ibid.*, **43**: 544–546, 1937.
† For statements and proofs of these theorems see Boolos and Jeffrey, op. cit. (footnote on p. 134), chapters 15 and 16.

SOLUTIONS

SECTION 1.18

1. (*a*)–(*c*) are t, f, f.

2. (*a*) The argument is "(i) $(H \land M) \lor (\neg H \land T)$, (ii) $M \leftrightarrow T$, (iii) H, *so* (iv) T." A longer version of (ii) is "$(M \land T) \lor (\neg M \land \neg T)$." In a counterexample (iii) is t and the conclusion is f, so HT is tf, which makes premises (i) and (ii) have the truth values of "M" and "$\neg M$," respectively. Then in no case are both true; no case is a counterexample; the argument is valid.

   (*b*) Yes: in the ttt case for HTM the premises and conclusion are all true. To discover that case, note that in any case in which (i)–(iv) are all true, HT would be tt, so (i) and (ii) would both have the same truth value as "M," which must also be t to make (i)–(iv) all t.

4. In a counterexample, A_1 would be t and A_{100} f, to make "$A_1 \to A_{100}$" f. If all premises "$A_1 \to A_2$, $A_2 \to A_3$, ..., $A_{99} \to A_{100}$" are to be t, truth of anteced-

ents (starting with "A_1") forces the consequent to be t as well. Eventually that makes "A_{100}" t; but it has to be f to make the conclusion f. Then there are no counterexamples; the argument is valid.

6. (a) "$A \rightarrow C, A \rightarrow \neg C$, so $\neg A$." In a counterexample, "A" would have to be t to make the conclusion f, but then one premise or the other would have to be f, since one of them must have a false consequent. No counterexamples; valid.

   (b) "$C \rightarrow A, \neg C$, so $\neg A$." Invalid; the tf case for AC is a counterexample.

7. (a)–(h) are f, t, f, f, t, f, t, t.

9. It's bad news for that view, since it's "$\neg (A \vee B)$" that's logically equivalent to "$\neg A \wedge \neg B$"; "$\neg (A \veebar B)$" is logically equivalent to a weaker sentence, "$(\neg A \wedge \neg B) \vee (A \wedge B)$."

10. (b) It's t iff an *odd* number of letters are t. That generalizes, e.g., "$[(A \veebar B) \veebar (C \veebar D)] \veebar (E \veebar F)$," with six letters, all distinct, is a way of saying that an odd number of them are t. Grouping and order don't matter; e.g., "$(B \veebar D) \veebar [(C \veebar A) \veebar (E \veebar F)]$" says the same thing.

    (c) If English disjunctions were basically exclusive, we'd naturally interpret ungrouped "A or B or C or D or E" as saying that an odd number of the components are true, which we certainly don't.

11. (c) The argument "$A \vee B$, so $\neg A \rightarrow B$" is valid and sensible, without the second premise "$\neg B$." From premises "$A \vee B, \neg B$" the immediate conclusion is "A," whence "$\neg A \rightarrow B$" follows validly—but inanely, since "A" itself is shorter, clearer, and more informative.

    (d) "(We advance $\rightarrow$ They withdraw) $\rightarrow$ We win, $\neg$We advance, so We win." That's valid: the second premise is t where the conclusion is f only in case ff for "We advance, We win." There the first premise is f, so there's no counterexample. But in the presence of the second premise the relevant reading of the first is the counterfactual one—on which the argument is invalid, since "We'd win, if they withdrew if we advanced" could be t when we neither advance nor win. Note: "We advance $\rightarrow$ They withdraw" is automatically t when the second premise is t, but "They'd withdraw if we advanced" says that the matter-of-fact conditional would remain t even if we made the second premise false.

12. Probabilities: (a) .8   (b) .4   (c) and (d) are logically equivalent.

13. Conditional probabilities: (a) 1/4   (b) 1/3   (c) 1/6

14. $pr (T \wedge N) = p$, $pr (T \vee N) = p + q + r$. If these are equal, $q + r = 0$. Since $p + q + r + s = 1$, this means that $p + s = 1$; and $p + s$ is $pr (T \leftrightarrow N)$. Answer: "100%."

15. H: He's a knight. I: I'm a knave. If the speaker, Vlad, is a knave (cases tt, ft for HI), what he says ("$H \vee I$") cannot be true: cases tt, ft are ruled out. If Vlad is not a knave (cases tf, ff), he's a knight, so "$H \vee I$" must be true, which rules out the ff case. The only possibility is tf, both knights.

16. No. If it were true, some Cretan would have said truly that all Cretans always lie, and that would have been no lie—so the Cretan prophet would have spoken truly.

SECTION 2.4

(g)
$$\checkmark (A \to B) \to C$$
$$\checkmark \neg(\neg C \to A)$$
$$\neg C$$
$$\neg A$$

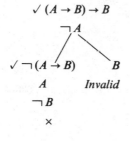

$$\checkmark \neg(A \to B) \qquad C$$
$$A \qquad \times$$
$$\neg B$$
$$\times \quad Valid$$

(h)
$$\checkmark (A \to B) \to A$$
$$\neg A$$

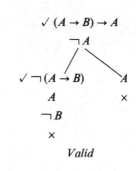

$$\checkmark \neg(A \to B) \qquad A$$
$$A \qquad \times$$
$$\neg B$$
$$\times$$
$$Valid$$

(i)
$$\checkmark (A \to B) \to B$$
$$\neg A$$

$$\checkmark \neg(A \to B) \qquad B$$
$$A \qquad Invalid$$
$$\neg B$$
$$\times$$

(j)
$$\checkmark A \to B$$
$$\checkmark B \to C$$
$$\checkmark C \to D$$
$$\checkmark \neg(A \to D)$$
$$A$$
$$\neg D$$

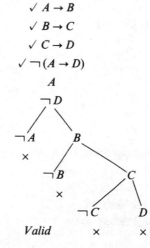

$$\neg A \qquad B$$
$$\times$$
$$\neg B \qquad C$$
$$\times$$
$$\neg C \qquad D$$
$$Valid \qquad \times \qquad \times$$

(k)

$\checkmark \neg H \to M$	(premise)
$W \to \neg H$	(premise)
$\checkmark \neg[\neg H \to (\neg W \to M)]$	($\neg$ conclusion)
$\neg H$	(from
$\checkmark \neg(\neg W \to M)$	line 3)
$\neg W$	(from
$\neg M$	line 5)

$$\neg\neg H \qquad M \qquad \text{(from line 1)}$$
$$\times \qquad \times$$

Valid (Note that we didn't need the second premise.)

SECTION 2.5

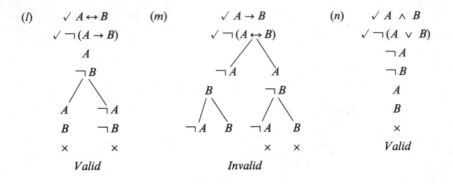

(*l*)　　$\checkmark\ A \leftrightarrow B$　　(*m*)　　　$\checkmark\ A \rightarrow B$　　(*n*)　　$\checkmark\ A \wedge B$

　　　$\checkmark\ \neg(A \rightarrow B)$　　　　$\checkmark\ \neg(A \leftrightarrow B)$　　　　$\checkmark\ \neg(A \vee B)$

　　　　　A　　　　　　　　　　　　　　　　　　　$\neg A$

　　　　　$\neg B$　　　　　　$\neg A$　　　A　　　　$\neg B$

　　　A　　$\neg A$　　　B　　　$\neg B$　　　　A

　　　B　　$\neg B$　　$\neg A$　B　$\neg A$　B　　B

　　　$\times$　　$\times$　　　$\times$　　$\times$　　　　$\times$

　　　　Valid　　　　　　　*Invalid*　　　　　　*Valid*

SECTION 3.4

(*d*)　　　　$\neg Lab$　　　(*e*)　　$\forall x\ Lxa$　　(*f*)　　$\forall x\ (Lxa \rightarrow Lax)$

　　　$\checkmark\ \neg\neg \forall x\ Lxb$　　　　$\neg Laa$　　　　　$\neg Lab$

　　　　$\forall x\ Lxb$　　　　　　Laa　　　　　　$\neg\neg Lba$

　　　　　Lab　　　　　　　$\times$　　　　$\checkmark\ (Lba \rightarrow Lab)$

　　　　　$\times$

　　　　　　　　　　　　　　　　　　　$\neg Lba$　　　Lab

　　　　　　　　　　　　　　　　　　　$\times$　　　　$\times$

All are valid. Note that in (*f*) the tree closes without applying the rule for double denials to line 3—itself, the denial of "$\neg Lba$" at the lower left.

(*g*)

1	$\forall x\ (Mx \rightarrow H)$	(premise)	
2	$\checkmark\ \neg(\exists x\ Mx \rightarrow H)$	($\neg$ conclusion)	$\neg(O \rightarrow \Delta)$
3	$\checkmark\ \exists x\ Mx$	(from 2)	O
4	$\neg H$	(from 2)	$\neg \Delta$
5	Ma	(from 3—"by EI" goes without saying)	
6	$\checkmark\ (Ma \rightarrow H)$	(from 1—" by UI" goes without saying)	
7	$\neg Ma$　　H	(from 6)	

　　　　$\times$　　$\times$

　　　　　Valid

SECTION 4.10

1. Yes. The tree can be simpler than that of Example 4.8.

2. No. The tree has five lines.

3. No.

4. Yes. Line numbers go up to 8.

5. No. It's an 11-line tree.

6. Yes; 10 lines.

7. Yes; 12 lines.

8. Yes; 14 lines.

9. Yes; a 10- and an 11-line tree.

10. (*a*) No. (*b*) None of Alma's lovers' lovers love her.

SECTION 4.12

1. Obviously not. The first three lines of the (infinite) tree are

$$\forall x \; Lxa, \; \neg \exists x \; \forall y \; Lxy, \; \forall x \; \neg \forall y \; Lxy$$

They continue

$$Laa, \; \neg \forall y \; Lay, \; \exists y \; \neg Lay, \; \neg Lab, \; Lba, \; \neg \forall y \; Lby, \; \exists y \; \neg Lby, \; \neg Lbc,$$

and in general, where *name*$_1$ is "*a*," *name*$_2$ is "*b*," etc.,

$$L \; name_i a, \; \neg \forall y \; L \; name_i y, \; \exists y \; \neg L \; name_i y, \; \neg L \; name_i name_{i+1}$$

Counterexample.

Domain: $\{1, 2, \ldots\}$.

Extension of *name*$_i$: the number i.

Extension of "*L*": $\{(1, 1), (2, 1), (3, 1), (4, 1), (5, 1), \ldots\}$.

2. All but (*a*), for which the domain of the counterexample is $\{1, 2\}$, extensions of "*a*" and "*b*" are 1 and 2, extension of "*P*" is $\{1\}$. In this interpretation, "$\forall x \; (Px \to \forall y \; Py)$" has the same truth value as the conjunction "$(Pa \to \forall y \; Py) \wedge (Pb \to \forall y \; Py)$," where the first conjunct is false since 1 is in $\{1\}$ (true antecedent) but 2 isn't (false consequent).

3. No; (i) implies (ii) but not vice versa.

4. No; (ii) implies (i) but not vice versa.

SECTION 4.17

1. (a) $\exists x \, [Tx \, \wedge \, \forall y \, (Gy \to Fyx)]$
   (b) $\forall x \, [Gx \to \exists y \, (Ty \, \wedge \, Fxy)]$
2. (a) $\forall x \, [(Gx \, \wedge \, \neg \exists y \, Fxy) \to \forall y \, (Ty \to Lxy)]$
   (b) $\exists x \, Tx$
   (c) $\forall x \, \{[Gx \, \wedge \, \exists y \, (Ty \, \wedge \, Lxy)] \to \forall y \, Fyx\}$
   (d) $\exists y \, (Ty \, \wedge \, Lay)$
   (e) $Ga \to \forall x \, Fxa$

SECTION 5.10

5. (a) $Lab \, \wedge \, \forall z \, (Laz \to z = b)$, or $\forall z \, (Laz \leftrightarrow z = b)$
   (b) $Lab \, \wedge \, \forall z \, (Lzb \to z = a)$, or $\forall z \, (Lzb \leftrightarrow z = a)$
   (c) $\exists x \, [Lxx \, \wedge \, \forall z \, (Lxz \to z = x)]$, or $\exists x \, \forall z \, (Lxz \leftrightarrow z = x)$
   (d) $\forall x \, \{[Tx \, \wedge \, \neg \exists y \, (Gy \, \wedge \, y \neq a \, \wedge \, Fxy)] \to Fxa\}$
   (e) $\exists x \, \{[Tx \, \wedge \, \neg \exists y \, (Gy \, \wedge \, y \neq a \, \wedge \, Fxy)] \, \wedge \, Fxa\}$
   (f) $\exists y \, (Fya \, \wedge \, \forall x \, \{[Tx \, \wedge \, \neg \exists y \, (Gy \, \wedge \, y \neq a \, \wedge \, Fxy)] \leftrightarrow x = y\})$
6. (i) $Ga \, \wedge \, \forall x \, \{[Tx \, \wedge \, \neg \exists y \, (Gy \, \wedge \, y \neq a \, \wedge \, Fxy)] \to Fxa\}$
   (ii) $\forall x \, [Tx \to \exists y \, (Gy \, \wedge \, Fxy)] \to \forall x \, (Tx \to Fxa)$
7. (i) $\forall x \, \{[Gx \, \wedge \, \exists y \, (y \neq x \, \wedge \, Gx \, \wedge \, Fxy)] \to Lxx\}$
   (ii) $Ga \, \wedge \, \forall x \, (Fxa \, \wedge \, \neg Lxa)$, or $Ga \, \wedge \, \forall x \, Fxa \, \wedge \, \forall x \, \neg Lxa$, etc.

SECTION 6.6

1. The tree has a single path, which grows forever. Since no identity sentences appear as lines, the extensions of the names "a," "fa," "ffa," "$fffa$," etc., in the interpretation C determined by this path are the same as their old extensions: 1, 2, 3, 4, etc. The predicate "P" is true of all but the first of these; its extension is the set $\{2, 3, 4, \ldots\}$. The extension of f is the successor function $1 +$.

2. The tree has a single path, which grows forever. All names "a," "fa," "ffa," etc., have the same extension in the interpretation C determined by this path; that'll be 1, the smallest number that's the old extension of any of those names. Then the extension of "f" is a function with 1 as its only argument and only value, i.e., the identity function, $id(1) = 1$.

SECTION 6.8

G5:

1	$g(b, a) \neq g(a, b)$	($\neg$G5)
2	$g(a, g(b, fb)) = g(g(a, b), fb)$	(G1)
3	$g(b, fb) = a$	(G3)
4	$g(a, a) = a$	(G2)
5	$a = g(g(a, b), fb)$	(3, 4, 2)
6	$g(b, fb) = g(g(a, b), fb)$	(3, 5)
7	$\checkmark\ g(b, fb) = g(g(a, b), fb) \to b = g(a, b)$	(G4)

8	$g(b, fb) \neq g(g(a, b), b)$	$b = g(a, b)$	(7)
9	$\times$	$g(b, a) = b$	(G2)
10		$g(b, a) = g(a, b)$	(8, 9)
		$\times$

G6:

1	$\checkmark\ \neg\ [\forall x\ g(x, b) = x \to b = a]$	($\neg$G6)
2	$\forall x\ g(x, b) = x$	(1)
3	$b \neq a$	(1)
4	$g(a, b) = a$	(2)
5	$g(b, a) = g(a, b)$	(G5)
6	$g(b, a) = a$	(4, 5)
7	$g(b, a) = b$	(G2)
8	$b = a$	(6, 7)
	$\times$	

G7: Use the new name from $\checkmark\ \neg$G7 to instantiate G1, G3, G5, G4.

G8: G1, G7, G3, G1, G3, G7, G2, G5

G9: Use G8.

SECTION 7.2

4.

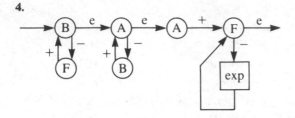

If the "exp" program of problem 3 leaves y^x, y, 0, 0, 0 in register A when started with x, y, 0, 0, 0 in registers A–E, this program leaves $\sup(x, y)$ in A when started with x, y, 0, 0, 0, 0, in A–F.

SECTION 7.6

1. (a) Running time of this one is $2n + 1$, so $r(n + 1) \geq 2n + 1$.

(b) Fig. 7.6b shows that $r(n) < r(n + 1)$, so ...

(c) If R computes r, there will be $r[r(n)]$ stones in register A when this program halts, and as it takes a passage through a node to put a stone into a register, the running time of this program is at least $r[r(n)]$, and the program has $r(n + k + 2)$ nodes.

(d) If a k-node program R exists that computes r, then by problem 1c, $r(n + k + 2) \geq r[r(n)]$ for all n, so by problem 1b, $n + k + 2 \geq r(n)$ for all n, and thus $n + 1 + k + 2 \geq r(n + 1)$ for all n, and by problem 1a, $n + 1 + k + 2 \geq 2n + 1$ for all n. Simplifying, $k + 2 \geq n$ for all n, so that $k > n$ for all n, which implies $k > k$, $0 > 0$, and other absurdities.

2. It suffices to specify something that would be a mechanical procedure for computing r if there were a register machine program H for computing the function h. Here is such a procedure, based on the fact that among the programs P_0, P_1, P_2, ... only a finite number $P_{i+1}, \ldots, P_{i+N}$ have exactly n nodes. On N machines, simultaneously start these N programs, with all registers but A initially empty, and with A initially containing the numbers $i + 1, \ldots, i + N$, respectively. On N other machines, simultaneously start the program H, with all registers but A initially empty, and with A initially containing the numbers $i + 1, \ldots, i + N$, respectively. As each of the first N machines halts, note what the running time has been. (Not all will halt.) After the last of the second N machines has halted (as they will, eventually), note whether or not all the first N that ever will halt have done so. If so, you know the running time of the longest-running of them, i.e., $r(n)$. If not, just wait until the time comes (as it must, sooner or later) when those that are still running, but for which the corresponding H programs have produced the value 0, have halted. *Then* you will know the value $r(n)$. As this procedure is purely mechanical, the Church-Turing thesis assures us that if H existed, some program would compute r. As no program can compute r, H does not exist.

SECTION 8.8

1. The problem is equivalent to the decision problem for consistency of finite sets of ∃∀ sentences without function symbols, a problem that's solvable because reducible to problem II, which we know to be solvable. (If there are n existential quantifiers in the ∃∀ sentences, n applications of EI yield a set of ∀ sentences that is consistent or not depending on whether or not the set of ∃∀ sentences is consistent.)

SECTION 9.9

1. As $EG(\bigcirc/D)$ contains no nonlogical constants, its truth value in an interpretation depends only on the size of that interpretation's domain, not on the particular individuals in it.

2. The interpretations in which Q1 and Q2 are both true are those whose domains include the enumerable infinity of extensions of the names "0," "$s0$," "$ss0$," etc.—perhaps with other individuals as well. The presence of "∃Q" in $EG(\bigcirc/D)$ means that the whole domain needn't be enumerably infinite; it's enough that it contain an enumerably infinite set.

3. The sentence $\bigcirc$ is consistent iff its conjunction with the logical truth "$\forall x\, \exists y\, (Kx \rightarrow Ky)$" is.